The Right Way To
Write Reports

The Right Way To Write Reports

Steve Gravett

RIGHT WAY

Typeset in 10½/11½ pt Times by Letterpart Ltd, Reigate, Surrey.

Printed and bound in Great Britain by Cox & Wyman Ltd, Reading, Berkshire.

The *Right Way* series is published by Elliot Right Way Books, Brighton Road, Lower Kingswood, Tadworth, Surrey, KT20 6TD, U.K. For information about our company and the other books we publish, visit our web site at www.right-way.co.uk

CONTENTS

ACKNOWLEDGEMENTS

Hampshire Police Authority: *Annual Policing Policy Plan 1997-1998*

League Against Cruel Sports: *Deer and Staghunting*

Office of Fair Trading: *How to Get the Best Deal*

Autocar 25 June 1997: *VW Plans Polo Spider Spin-off*

Mr R B Culshaw, Director of Social Services, Isle of Wight Council: *New Horizons*

BBC: *Our Commitment to You – BBC Statement of Promises to Viewers and Listeners*

Part One

WHY REPORT?

1

WHAT IS A REPORT?

What is its Purpose?

The term *report* indicates a document with weight and authority. It conveys the impression to the reader of being well researched, carefully thought out, balanced, objective and impartial. It has a clear purpose, is organised systematically and targets a specific audience. (In the case of a technical report the readership may need some specialised knowledge to understand the contents.)

In the business world, or with public bodies and voluntary organisations, reports are requested prior to managers taking important decisions that affect personnel or involve sizeable expenditure.

On the other hand, a school report gives very specific information about how the student is performing. This is valuable to parents and to professional teaching staff.

The magazine *Which?* produces carefully researched reports on products available on the market, to inform its readers of the relative merits, qualities and value for money of competing consumer goods.

Some reports are written to help individuals and managers take crucial decisions about issues that affect them. They should address the main issues, reach conclusions and provide sufficient information for the reader to make an informed decision.

Reports vary in length from a short account of the Black-headed Bunting for the Natural History and Archaeological Society, to a report running into hundreds of pages produced by the Monopolies Commission or some other Government Inquiry Team.

The majority of reports will fall between these two extremes and will range from a few pages to possibly up to a hundred. The focus of this volume, and our attention, will be to concentrate on helping you to write whatever type of report you may be requested to provide.

Why are Reports Written?

Gone are the days when businesses or departments were small enough for decisions to be taken after a discussion between the manager and a specialist on the shop floor. Companies and organisations have expanded and are now increasingly dependent on documentation. This provides a record of decisions taken, and evidence that the issues have been analysed. Effective reports can enable management to retain the confidence of shareholders, directors and bankers.

One of the main advantages of a report is that it allows recipients the opportunity to study the contents and share the material with others. They can benefit from the advice of colleagues and have all the relevant information together at the same time. Unlike with verbal communications, the scope for misunderstanding is minimised by this process, especially when complex or technical issues are involved.

Scientists and technicians often perceive report writing as an unnecessary waste of their time. But the ability to communicate your findings, explain the importance of your research and obtain ongoing funding depends on this essential communication skill being mastered. Report writing is challenging. It obliges the writer to be self disciplined and set out the findings in a clear, logical manner without leaving them open to challenge and questioning from others.

Keep in mind the interests and needs of the intended readership all the time.

Reports fall broadly into five main types:

1. For the record.
This type of report is similar to the minutes of a meeting, whose purpose is to record the main points of a discussion and any decisions reached. It acts as an aide-mémoire. Professional people dealing with clients file reports for the case file, as a record of their contact and of the main issues discussed. It is permanently

available for future reference and consultation by other colleagues should they leave or be temporarily unavailable. A report filed at the time also has standing as an accurate account of events should the facts be later challenged. Compiling a report can be a form of insurance when a culture of blame develops in an organisation. It 'covers your back' in the sense there is evidence to say that you took appropriate action, always useful if things go wrong later! Auditors find corroborative evidence such as reports valuable when verifying, for example, the authenticity of travel claims.

2. To provide information.

Progress reports may be requested at specified intervals to keep managers and other interested parties appraised of the progress of a project. This can range from a banker requiring up-dated reports on a business to a committee seeking a routine departmental report from its Director. The primary purpose may be simply to keep people 'in the picture' about what is going on. This has many advantages: it heads off criticism, helps to maintain staff interest and motivation, and can become an investment for the future if you run into difficulties and need further help.

3. To help solve a problem.

Some reports are compiled to address a particular question or problem that has arisen which requires a carefully crafted response. Normally such reports are initiated by setting out clearly the 'terms of reference'. This will determine the structure and type of report required. For example:

'Provide a report to the Managing Director explaining why the volume of sales has fallen in the last quarter compared to the previous quarterly returns.'

This type of report is straightforward to prepare and might be fairly short.

4. To influence or persuade and attract publicity.

Some reports written by pressure groups or commercial bodies are designed to generate the maximum amount of publicity for a product or cause. A professional survey which produces startling results will be of interest to the media who will consider it newsworthy.

Any report setting out to influence public opinion has to be handled carefully if it is to have impact and credibility, otherwise the process is likely to back-fire.

5. *To assist the decision-making process.*
Public bodies frequently commission reports to seek advice from the officials of the authority on dealing with particular problems and issues.

In Local Government a Committee might ask its officials to consider and evaluate a whole range of options relating to a controversial issue like the proposed path of a by-pass around a village, or to evaluate the respective merits of building a Community Centre or a Sports Centre on land it owns, for the local community.

Central Government tends to produce 'Green Papers' to explore publicly the range of options available on a given topic and seek representations from interested groups. This is followed up by a 'White Paper' which sets out the Government's plans prior to introducing legislation.

The Board of Directors of a company may require the Chief Executive to evaluate the commercial aspects of a particular course of action and submit a report containing his proposals and recommendations.

Reports are frequently requested when managers or committees feel the need to seek advice on a topic that is complicated and needs a specialist or professional input.

For Whom are you Writing?
It is important to be clear who are your readers. The report may be written for a particular senior executive but it is likely that a range of other people will see it. Consider their needs, and the use that will be made of your report. Writing for a professional audience familiar with the company's products requires a different approach from the report written for shareholders or the general public.

An Annual Report prepared for the local Scouts group will have a wider secondary readership as it will be read by family and friends of the children involved.

The presentation of your material is important. The busy manager will be anxious to receive a report that is brief, clear, focused and in a style that is easy to read.

Most managers are inundated with reading material and develop a range of techniques for keeping on top of the growing pile of reports and documents that are required reading. They can cope only by being selective about how much they read and what to discard! Make your report user-friendly, otherwise it will not only find its way into the pending tray, but stay there!

The harassed and busy manager will concentrate on the following:

- Reading the headings and scanning the index, if one is included.
- Glancing through the contents to get the flavour of the report.
- Reading the Introduction and Executive Summary. This may be sufficient to appreciate the contents.
- Making notes of the key points as he works through the report. There may be insufficient time for a second reading.

Your report should be well structured with a clear and logical sequence, tightly written avoiding verbiage, and signposted so the reader can follow your argument logically. If the reader can appreciate its relevance to the business, he will want to allocate sufficient time to reading it thoroughly.

Understanding the Reader's Needs
Reading a report can be a daunting experience unless it conforms to certain expectations of the reader. It must be user-friendly, written in a clear, easily understood language and in a natural style. Otherwise the recipient will resist the idea of spending time wading through it. This natural resistance is known as the 'cognitive cost'.

A technical, closely typed report, written in a ponderous style, without illustrations, will have a high cognitive cost. It is clearly going to be hard work absorbing the contents.

On the other hand, a well illustrated, clearly written document, presented in an inviting fashion which appears easy to read, will have a low cognitive cost and be tackled with enthusiasm.

Let us examine your readers' needs systematically:

- *How user-friendly is the report?*
  The report should be structured with a contents list, subject headings, a summary and appropriate illustrations. Attention must be paid to the layout, with wide margins and double spacing to make it more readable.

- *Is the meaning clear?*
  Clarity is vital. Pay attention to the correct usage of words. Ensure phrases are unambiguous, and that sentences are not too long or confusing.

- *Can it be easily understood?*
  Avoid being verbose. Eliminate tedious explanations. Keep to the point and use simple, well known words, precise phrases and short, succinct sentences. Be generous with the use of paragraphs as these add impact and keep the reader's interest.

- *Is the style natural?*
  The report must flow if it is to be readable. Ensure that each point leads naturally on to the next and that the argument develops in a logical manner. Although a degree of formality is necessary, avoid impersonal, old-fashioned, bureaucratic style. But do not go to the other extreme and be over familiar or chatty. This will strike the wrong note.

Your readers will not appreciate your writing if you fall into the following bad habits:

- Politically incorrect phrases will offend some readers and get their backs up. This is an area where sensitivity is needed.
- Any bias that comes across will immediately devalue your report. It is wiser to avoid stating your personal views. Restrict yourself to explaining the alternatives objectively. Allow the readers to reach their own conclusions.

- Do not patronise your readers by talking down to them or being condescending. Assume they are intelligent and wish to be informed.

2

TYPES OF REPORT

Different Types of Report

There are literally hundreds of different types of report that are needed from time to time. In this chapter, I deal with the three that arise most commonly, and I give some principles for conducting an inquiry or investigation.

An Annual Report

Registered charities, Public Companies and many other bodies have to publish accounts and hold an Annual General Meeting each year.

The accounts are often incorporated into an Annual Report which usually accompanies and amplifies the Agenda for the AGM. It may follow this format, an example taken from the Annual Report of a Housing Association.

- *The Contents* list is self explanatory.
- *The Chairman's Report* is an overview of the previous year's work and acknowledges publicly the work of key members of the Board.
- *The Chief Executive's Report* is a review of the work of the Association and the achievements of the staff in the previous twelve months.
- *Supported Housing Schemes.* This section gives a detailed account of the supported schemes in each geographical area.
- *Tenant Participation* outlines the tenant participation strategy that the Board introduced and explains the policy and practice of the Tenants' Association.

- *Investing in People* details progress the Board has made towards achieving a varied and comprehensive training programme for all its staff.
- *New Homes into Management* describes how the Association has entered into a partnership arrangement with another Association and now manages two recently acquired hostels which cater for the needs of young people.
- *The Statistics section* illustrates graphically the housing stock, average rent levels, staffing, training costs, the ethnic origin of staff, the level of staff turnover, the repairs service response, details of lettings and empty properties.
- *The Balance Sheet* details the fixed assets, current assets, creditors, provisions for liabilities and charges, the share capital and level of reserves.
- *Income and Expenditure* provides a record of the turnover and surplus or deficit on ordinary activities, before and after taxation.
- *The Board of Management* gives personal details about the Board members, co-opted members and the Management Team.
- *Key Partners* acknowledges the work of key organisations, the Auditors, other professional advisers and technical consultants.

A Report for the Chief Executive

In a company the Chief Executive is the senior elected executive officer with day-to-day responsibility for running a business. He is accountable to the Chairman and the Board of Directors who formulate policy and provide guidance to the organisation's operational management. The Chief Executive leads a team of senior managers who are supported by their foremen, supervisors and others operating through a hierarchical structure.

In Local Government the Chief Executive is the most senior paid official who is accountable directly to the Council. The Council is made up of elected councillors. The most influential of these are normally chairmen of their individual committees. The most senior manager of each department is usually called a Director. Thus you could have a Director of Social Services reporting to the Social Services Committee, a Director of Education reporting to the Education Committee and likewise for

Planning, Highways, Recreation and Tourism Departments. Each Director works under the direction of the Chief Executive who co-ordinates their work on behalf of the Council.

Preparing a report for the Chief Executive of a company, or the Local Authority, is a responsible task requiring drafting skills and expertise. The layout of the required report will vary according to convention and the house style of the company or Council involved. However, the approach adopted is similar:

- *Preparation* involves considering the terms of reference and purpose, the scope of the report and the intended reader- ship.
- *Research and collecting data* is the next step which may involve researching and interviewing customers, the general public and service providers by means of questionnaires, and collating the results.
- *Structuring the report* involves analysing the information gathered and presenting it in the following layout:
  a) Introduction
  b) An Executive Summary
  c) The Main Report
  d) Conclusions
  e) Recommendations
  f) Appendices
- *Writing the report* will involve drafting and redrafting, before preparing the final version complete with graphs and other types of illustration.
- *Submitting the report* may include designing the layout and arranging for it to be printed, ensuring it is completed by the agreed deadline.

The Committee Report
Most organisations, whether they be voluntary or charitable, a business or a Local Authority, have a structure which includes committees. In a business there is a Board of Directors and a number of operating committees, depending on the size of the company. Voluntary organisations, charities, clubs and societies have some form of management committee or council to oversee activities. Public bodies and Local Authorities all have an elabo- rate committee structure which includes sub-committees and an

internal structure of accountability. Every committee has to be serviced and this involves officials and office holders in the preparation of reports.

The following example shows the format of a report prepared for the Council by the Chairman of the Tourism Committee, with the help of departmental officials:

- *The Foreword* outlines the attractions of this seaside resort which is described as a 'highly marketable tourism product'.
- *The Executive Summary* succinctly summarises the whole report and strongly endorses the overall strategy recommended to the Council.
- *The Introduction* provides a brief overview, outlines the need for and purpose of the strategy, and describes the methodology adopted.
- *Review of the Resort's Tourism Product* identifies the intrinsic qualities, the commercial attractions, accommodation and transportation issues affecting tourism in the town.
- *The Current Market Position and Trends* is an analysis of visitor characteristics, occupancy data and trends.
- *Strengths and weaknesses* is an analysis of the resort's attributes and shortcomings.
- *Key Threats and Market Opportunities* examines external pressures and market opportunities, and looks at developmental opportunities in the medium term.
- *The Strategy* outlines the general principles, objectives, proposals for action and the priorities for the proposed action plan.
- *Conclusion and Recommendations* comprises a succinct summary and outlines the benefits to the resort over the next decade by adopting this strategy. This section often includes an Action Plan and differs from the Executive Summary which concentrates on the main overall thrust of the report.

Conducting an Inquiry

An Inquiry is usually held to examine a problem which is causing serious concern. Its purpose is to establish what needs to be done to improve the situation by analysing the causes and identifying options to improve matters. Inquiries are sometimes triggered when an incident occurs which points the finger at an underlying problem and serves as the catalyst to examine it.

Conducting one and subsequently preparing a report demands a systematic approach. The key to success is to answer the following questions methodically:

- What is the purpose of the Inquiry?
- Who will conduct it?
- What methodology will be used to:
  a) gather relevant information,
  b) consider and evaluate the relevant facts,
  c) make appropriate recommendations?
- How will the final report be prepared?

The facts, the sequence of events, and lessons to be learned, need to be established.

The final report should cover:

- The circumstances that led up to the incident occurring.
- What actually happened, and the sequence of events.
- Why the incident occurred.
- Action taken in response to the incident and how effective it was.
- Further follow-up action that has been taken since the incident.
- Action taken or planned to prevent a recurrence.

The format adopted for the final report should contain:

1. An account of the nature of the Inquiry and the methodology used.
2. A description and analysis of what happened.
3. The conclusions reached and a series of recommendations which:
   a) Identify any need for a change in policy, practice or procedure.
   b) Identify any action by staff which is praiseworthy or a cause for concern.

c)   Consider the appropriateness of any disciplinary action which should be fully examined and high-lighted.
4.   The appendix which should include any other material relevant to the Inquiry, together with any records of inter-views carried out.

The Inquiry report should be submitted to the manager who initiated it and who will have to decide what follow-up action is necessary. This may require consultation with other senior per-sonnel before any agreed recommendations can be implemented.

Example
This outline sketches the structure of an Inquiry which was conducted into the standard of care in a privately registered residential home, following a rise in the number of complaints received.

- *The Preface* serves as an Executive Summary.
- *The Introduction* outlines the scope of the Inquiry.
- *Contents* list.
- *The Historical Background* gives a potted history of the establishment and summarises previous inspection reports.
- *What We Were Told* recounts the views of the Officer-in-Charge, Residential Care Staff, the Proprietor and the rel-evant staff association.

This is followed by reflections on the above briefings by the Inquiry team.

- *What We Found* is a factual account of practice observed, including how care staff and managers behave and an evaluation of the quality of life provided for the residents. The team examine the scope of health care offered, the quality of accommodation, the standards of care provided for the residents, taking into account their views and expe-riences.
- *The Conclusion* assesses the lack of progress made since the last inspection and the continuing level of concern about falling standards.

- *Recommendations and Examples of Best Practice* were divided into recommendations for the Officer-in-Charge of the home to take forward, recommendations for the Proprietors of this privately run home and advice to the Director of Social Services in whose area the home was registered.

3

PROPOSALS, LETTERS, MEMOS AND MINUTES

Though these are not reports in the sense outlined in the last chapter, they require the same skills. The report writer will often come across them, or need to do them, as part of normal work.

Writing a Proposal
A proposal is designed to sell a product, service, idea or solution. Its purpose is to generate extra business and increase profitability. As with any report, it should be clear, easy to read and succinct. Its aim is to persuade the prospective customer to do business with you by accepting your product or your proposed solution to their problem.

Here is a suggested format for writing a proposal for the purchase of a washing machine.

1. *Introduction*: This articulates your qualifications and relevant experience. Defines the problem facing the customer.
2. *Discussion*: Sets out your understanding of the customer's requirements. Analyses all possible options including the pros and cons of each machine on the market.
    Outlines the methodology that will be used and explains how comparisons will be made.
3. *Analysis*: Identifies a range of washing machines on the market that conform with the customer's basic requirements and fall within the preferred price range.
4. *Evaluation*: This section makes an evaluation based on comparative data and answers questions like:

Which machine gives the whitest wash?

What features does each machine have?

How useful are they to the customer?

It provides a features checklist and considers the value of: pre-set programmes, an extra rinsing facility, care symbols, the spin-alone option, built-in delay timers, the rinse and hold feature, and the necessity for an immediate door release feature. This might be in chart form.

5. *Conclusions*: Assesses the overall performance and reliability of washer-driers.

Reaches conclusions about which features are likely to be beneficial.

Considers which machine represents best value for money.

6. *Recommendation*: This contains a short list of suitable machines, from which the customer can make a final selection.

The nature of proposals vary and depend on the customer's needs. For instance, a Government Department may have specific requirements and demand answers to a series of detailed questions.

The following structure is a suitable format for preparing a proposal for an organisation.

Management Summary:

a)   Briefly states what is being proposed, including the costs involved and the timescale.

b)   Identifies the main advantages of your proposal.

c)   Assesses the value of your proposed solution for the customer.

Description of Problem:

a)   Outlines the background to the problem.

b)   Demonstrates your understanding of the problem.

c)   Specifies what needs to be done.

Possible solutions:

a)   Sets out a range of options.

b)   Evaluates the strengths and weaknesses of the alternatives.

c)   Demonstrates your expertise and knowledge of possible solutions.

Recommended option:
a)   Describes in detail your proposed solution.
b)   Presents attractively the benefits of your proposal.

Cost analysis:
a)   A full breakdown of the costs involved.
b)   Any stage payments required.
c)   Identifies extra costs that may be involved.
d)   Includes any optional extras that may be incurred.

Appendices:
a)   Technical and legal specifications.
b)   Product descriptions and brochures.
c)   Statistical information.
d)   Financial statements.

The Business Letter

Letters are used to provide a customer with a quotation or to confirm an order or a booking. They act as a permanent record of the writer's intentions. They have legal standing in a court of law if there is a dispute about the terms of an order, the price or specification.

There is no universally accepted way to lay out a business letter, although larger companies use headed paper and may have a distinct house style.

The following information should be included in a business letter:

- your address
- your telephone, fax and e-mail numbers
- a charity reference number, company registration number and/or your VAT registration number.

The above are usually printed on a business letterhead, then the following are typed in:

- the date
- the recipient's name
- your reference number.

It is important to include the correct full name and address of the customer on the left hand side of the letter. Not only does this ensure you can use a window envelope, but it provides a record of the customer's address on your copy of the correspondence.

There are several standard opening forms of address for a business letter:

- *Dear Sir* is impersonal and is not advised. Only use it if you cannot find out the name of your correspondent.
- *Dear Mr/Mrs/Miss/Ms/Dr* is the normal, formal style of address adopted by most organisations and companies. The use of *Ms* is correct if you either do not know a woman's marital status or have not established how she prefers to be addressed.
- *Dear Jack/Anne* is an informal, friendly form of opening used when writing to a business colleague with whom you have a good relationship.

Ending letters is more straightforward:

- *Yours faithfully* is always used when you open the letter with Dear Sir.
- *Yours sincerely* is normally used when the recipient's name or title is included in the form of address, e.g. Dear Mr/Mrs/Miss/Ms/Dr.
- *Kind regards/Regards* is used to sign letters addressed to the individual by their Christian name.
- *Best wishes* is for close acquaintances.

The structure of a business letter should follow the format of a short report and includes the following:

- *An introduction* which explains concisely the reason for the letter.
- *The main paragraphs* which contain the essence of the communication. They may confirm an agreement reached, clarify the main issues that arose in discussion or simply share information you consider to be relevant.
- *The closing paragraph* requests action, confirmation that

the proposed arrangements are acceptable, etc., and explains how further contact can be made with the writer.

Now look at this correspondence:

The Old Mill
Lake Road
WINCHESTER
Hampshire
(Postcode)

1st January (year)

Court and King Ltd
New Forest Road
SOUTHAMPTON
Hampshire
(Postcode)

Dear Mr James

Washing Machine Proposal

Thank you for your proposal recommending an AEG washing machine as the most suitable for our needs.

I accept the price of £xxx for the OKO Lavamat 6100, plus £xx for delivery and installation, all including VAT.

Please supply, deliver and install it next Friday, 5th January, and invoice me.

Yours sincerely

J S Bleed

The reply:

Dear Mr Bleed

Thank you for your letter dated 1st January confirming your order. We will be pleased to supply and install this washing machine on Friday on receipt of your cheque for £xxx.

I look forward to hearing from you by return.

Yours sincerely

John James
COURT AND KING LTD

Clearly some misunderstanding has arisen between the customer and supplier. The customer thought he would be paying for the goods once they were delivered and installed. However, the supplier believed the agreement was that payment would be made first. This demonstrates the value of a confirmatory letter.

Sending a Memo (Memorandum)

Memoranda are for communications within an organisation. They are often short and usually deal with a single topic. Their scope can range from a one line reminder about a meeting or an appointment, to a lengthy account of a personnel problem that requires formal disciplinary action.

Memos require care in the choice of language and style adopted, with thought given to the reader's needs. The priority is to get your message across succinctly.

Structurally a memo follows the model of a good report, but will normally have a title which avoids the necessity for an introductory paragraph. A longer memo will have headings and sub-headings to capture the reader's interest and draw attention to the main substance.

A memo might take the form of an *aide-mémoire*, which is a reminder or briefing document. This will contain the main headings and points which can be expanded orally.

Memos are often copied to people other than the addressee, so normally included on the memo is a list of those who are to receive copies. Sometimes 'hidden' copies (also known as 'blind' copies) are sent to other people (including your line manager, if the matter reflects poorly on you) so care is needed about confidentiality. Marking a memo 'confidential' is likely to ensure it is widely read! Unless the circulation list is restricted, and the memos distributed in sealed envelopes, this form of communication tends to be fairly open!

Memos received are usually filed away, so the originator's details and reference should be included – especially if the correspondence is one of a series between managers and subordinates. Here is a good example of a memo, followed by one of an *aide-mémoire*:

MEMORANDUM

From	John Daniels	**Telephone**	(01345) 123456
	Sales Director	**Extension**	12
	Waterside Marina	**Date**	10-03-(year)
		Fax	(01345) 324516
To	All Sales Staff	**Your ref**	SALES/03
	Copies for information:	**Our ref**	RJF/PB
	The Managing Director		

Re: *Improved Facilities for the Coming Season*

We are rapidly approaching the new season and I am writing to all boat owners to remind them of the new facilities we have provided.

1.   The refurbished bar and restaurant open on 5th April and all customers qualify for a 10% discount during April.
2.   The company are introducing Boat Insurance this season as an additional service to boat owners. As an incentive to promote this service, all new business generated will earn you 15% commission.
3.   The shower block has been refurbished over the winter and we are fully stocked with gas bottles, diesel and petrol, and unleaded fuel is available for the first time.
4.   We still have pontoon moorings available and I would urge

you to promote them vigorously. Discounts apply for annual bookings.

AIDE-MEMOIRE

From John Ball   **Telephone**
                            Extension
To   Michael Groves   **Date**   23-04-(year)
                            Your ref
                            Our ref

Re: *Complaints Procedure*

Before we meet the complainant's solicitor I thought it would be helpful to remind you of the updated complaints procedure, which is as follows:

1. Complaints against the National Health Service must normally be made within 6 months of the incident occurring.
2. **First stage** is local resolution. Complaints are directed to the doctor, nurse, receptionist or Practice Manager.
3. **Second stage** is the Patient's Charter which entitles the complainant to a written reply within four weeks from the Chief Executive.
4. **Third stage** is an Independent Review, where the complaint can be referred to a Convenor who may set up a panel to investigate the matter.
5. **Fourth stage** involves the Health Service Commissioner or the Ombudsman who conducts an independent investigation into the complaint once other channels have been exhausted.
6. Complainants can at any time raise a complaint through their solicitor or MP.

This aide-mémoire is written to remind a colleague of the complaints procedure which has to be followed. Its purpose is as a checklist for use with the patient's solicitor, to establish the sequence of procedures needed to establish liability, which must be done before any negotiations can take place about possible compensation.

Taking Minutes

Formal meetings held between managers, managers and their teams, managers and union representatives, and formal customer meetings, are among those that need to be minuted. This creates a permanent record of the action agreed. It allows progress to be checked using the minutes as a tool to monitor performance.

The minutes of a meeting are often widely circulated and therefore need to be carefully worded to preserve any confidences, avoid ambiguity and convey a positive message.

All formal meetings should have a published agenda. This acts as the structure for the meeting and the resulting minutes. The minutes of the meeting should record the following information:

- who was present at the meeting
- where and when the meeting took place
- a record of the key issues discussed and a record of any decisions reached
- an action column to show who is taking forward any outstanding matter
- the date of the next meeting, if appropriate.

MANAGEMENT/STAFF ASSOCIATION MEETING

Venue: AJK Headquarters
Date: 14 April (year)
Time: 1400hrs

AGENDA

1. Apologies
2. Minutes of the last meeting
3. Matters Arising:
   Relocation Package
4. Redundancy Scheme for those over 55
5. Any other business
6. Date of the next meeting

MINUTES OF THE MANAGEMENT/STAFF ASSOCIATION MEETING

held at AJK Headquarters on 14 April (year) at 1400hrs.

Present: J Blakey, Managing Director (Chairman)
S Norris, Personnel Director
P Appleby, Financial Director
A Neart (Secretary)
Union Representatives: P Vale (Convenor)
                                       A Dash
                                       P Jewel

ACTION

1.   Apologies.
       None.
2.   Minutes of the last meeting.
       These were agreed and signed jointly by Mr
       Blakey and Mr Vale.
3.   Matters Arising.
       Mr Vale reported that the membership had
       considered the Relocation Package discussed
       at the last meeting and had agreed at a
       Branch Meeting held on 20 March to accept
       it.
       Mr Appleby said plans to relocate HQ from
       London to Birmingham were well advanced
       and the lease for the new building had been
       agreed.
4.   Redundancy Scheme.
       The Personnel Director had circulated a
       paper detailing the Redundancy Scheme for
       those over 55 who wished to take early sev-
       erance. The union felt the terms of the
       scheme in certain respects were deficient and
       would not be acceptable to the members
       without amendment. Mr Norris said further
       discussions could take place informally on
       points of concern. He stressed AJK would

prefer a voluntary early severance scheme
than have to resort to compulsory redundancies. It was agreed the Personnel Director and
Convenor would meet the union to discuss
their reservations and report back at the next   Mr Norris
meeting.   Mr Vale

5.   Any other business.

The Convenor asked when they would
receive a reply to their pay and productivity
claim submitted in February. Mr Appleby
said he was preparing a detailed response and
this would be sent to the Convenor shortly.   Mr Appleby

6.   Date of next meeting.

This was scheduled for 12 June at 1400hrs at
AJK Headquarters.

Part Two

GOOD WRITING

4

WRITING A GOOD REPORT

The Ingredients of a Good Report

The main ingredients of a good report are that it is user-friendly, written for its intended audience and achieves the author's purpose.

Clarity is all important, otherwise misunderstandings occur, confusion results and ambiguity creeps in. Focused writing is essential.

The report should not digress from the main point. Rambling or wordy reports are irritating to read and should be avoided at all costs.

Start with a clear set of objectives. Keep in mind who the readers are, and what they know about the subject matter. Keep their interest in the topic alive. Consider how the issues affect *them*, how strongly they are likely to feel, and how high the subject matter figures on their priority list.

A sound structure is vital if the report is to flow. Discipline yourself to achieve this by having a beginning, a middle and an end:

- *The beginning contains the introduction*, the terms of reference, methodology and executive summary.
- *The middle is the core of the document* and contains the report's message. This is where the evidence and findings are analysed. The main arguments are developed and the reader's interest, aroused earlier, is sustained.
- *The end contains the conclusions*. It explains them, how they have been arrived at, and lists recommendations for

further action. It also contains an Appendix of supporting documents.

Effective Communication

The art of communicating effectively is to develop a logical structure.

- *The report should flow* seamlessly and, en route, signpost its intentions whilst it progresses towards its climax.
- *Plenty of headings* and sub-headings break up the text visually, making the content easier to read and understand.
- *The use of appropriate language* is key to developing a relaxed, natural style. Short, snappy sentences. Compact paragraphs. Straightforward words. Simple phrases and descriptive language. All these help to make the message easily understood!
- *Careful editing* and redrafting will be repaid with a well-structured, readable, finished document, free of factual errors, non sequiturs and contradictions.
- *Good grammar*, correct punctuation, an absence of spelling mistakes and distracting typing errors, will reap dividends.

Examples of Good Practice

The following extract from 'New Horizons' is reproduced by kind permission of Mr R B Culshaw, Director of Social Services, Isle of Wight Council.

THE NEW MILLENNIUM

A Strategy for Developing Services in the Next Century.

1. Introduction

The Community and Social Services Department has been subject to significant changes over the past few years including the additional responsibility for meeting Housing needs, changes to the delivery of Child Care and the provision of Community Care Services.

It is becoming increasingly apparent that there needs to be a clear demarcation between the Purchaser and Provider

functions. The time is right for a change in approach and a
new structure should be created which:
a)   is flexible
b)   shares expertise across the directorate
c)   offers clear lines of responsibility
d)   sharpens accountability.
The proposed changes, outlined in the Appendix, create a
clear demarcation line between the Purchaser and Provider,
and this is referred to as an organic structure.

2. The Management Style
An organic approach will facilitate a more flexible style of
management. This can only be achieved by creating a
Strategic Framework which allocates responsibility and
accountability very specifically for the assessment and
delivery of services.

The new roles of Assistant Director for Commissioning
and Assistant Director of Health and Community Services,
are described more fully in the Appendix.

3. Management Groups
The responsibility for strategic direction within the Directorate will be the Assistant Director's and the Operations
Manager's. They will develop a strategy which is consistent
with the Council's overall policy and encourages the development of a high quality, needs based, Social Care and
Housing service.

This strategy will be taken forward by means of a partnership approach with the Area Health Authority, voluntary
organisations and community groups. They will pool their
knowledge and expertise in order to achieve agreed targets.

4. Accountability
This report recognises the need for clear lines of responsibility and accountability. There is a requirement for a
consistent response in line with current policy and agreed
priorities. Consistency is necessary in the following areas:
a)   the interpretation of policy
b)   equality of treatment and availability of the service to all
c)   the whole of the County.

5. Conclusions

The new Directorate will be 'action focused', and the overall strategy will result in a clear set of outcomes and objectives. Individual performances will be judged against the achievement of those targets.

The organisation of service groupings will be reviewed constantly to ensure the best response to the achievement of outcomes.

The policy of disseminating information on a 'need to know' basis will be frequently reviewed in order to encourage the free expression of views and opinions.

6. Recommendations

a)   The strategy outlined be adopted as policy by the Housing and Social Services Committee.

b)   A new Mission Statement be adopted called *"People Come First"*.

7. The Appendices

a)   Revised Departmental Structure
b)   Strategic Planning Group
c)   Operational Management Structure
d)   Person Specifications
e)   Revised Job Descriptions

See how this report follows the structure:

● *Beginning*: covers the Introduction
● *Middle*: covers Management Style, Management Groups, Accountability and develops the arguments.
● *End*: contains the Conclusions, Recommendations and Appendices

Is it an example of effective communication? Judge that by asking yourself the following questions:

1.   Does the report flow well?
2.   Is the argument for change developed logically?
3.   Are there enough headings?

4.   Is the content easy to follow and understand?
5.   Is the language appropriate?
6.   Does it avoid jargon or gobbledegook?
7.   Are there plenty of paragraphs?
8.   Are over-long sentences avoided?
9.   Is there an absence of factual errors and contradictions?
10.   Does the writer express him/herself clearly?
11.   Does the writer avoid punctuation mistakes and typographical errors?

The answers to all these questions should be 'yes' – the hallmark of an excellent report.

Here is another example, reproduced by kind permission of *Autocar*, from the issue of 25 June 1997:

VW PLANS TO LAUNCH NEW POLO SPIDER

New 120mph sporty roadster planned for 2001.

1. Introduction
VW plans to introduce a range of new models over the next few years in an attempt to lift sales to over four million annually. These plans include replacing the Corrado and Beetle, introducing a high specification supermini capable of doing 94 mpg (miles per gallon) and a stylish Polo-based sports car capable of outperforming the rival Fiat Barchetta and the new Mazda MX-5.

2. Image
This two seater roadster will be a well equipped sports car. The emphasis is on eye catching looks, driver enjoyment and a strong life-style image.

3. Production Plans
The Polo Spider will be produced in Woolfsburg on an initial production basis of 30,000 vehicles per annum. Its style is heavily influenced by the German coachbuilder Karman with input from the Woolfsburg-based design team headed by Hartmut Warkuss.

4. Specification
The car will be priced at a very competitive £14,000. This will be achieved by featuring a high percentage of high-cost components from other production models. This will ensure reliability and reduce development costs. The model will include a high specification including an on-board computer, power windows, central-locking, power-assisted steering and a sophisticated vehicle immo-biliser system.

5. Engine Details
VW's new 16 valve, 1.4 litre, four cylinder petrol engine will provide the power providing 100 bhp (brake horse power) at 5200 rpm (revolutions per minute) and 94 lb ft at 4400 rpm. Acceleration from 0-60 will take 9 seconds and its top speed of 120 mph will make this a sprightly, lively, economical car with 35 mpg expected from the average driver.

6. Conclusions
There is no doubt that rival car firms will be alarmed to hear of the impending arrival of the Polo Spider, with its high performance specification, enviable reputation for reliability and build quality, all for under £14,000. The possibility that VW intends to include a larger 116 bhp, 2.0 litre petrol engine in the range will make the Polo Spider a force to be reckoned with in the next century.

7. Recommendation
The Polo Spider offers 120 mph performance, sporty han-dling and modern styling all for under £14,000. Undoubt-edly excellent value for money for the motorist seeking a stylish and exciting car to complement their lifestyle in the 20th Century.

This report also conforms to the structure outlined earlier and contains many of the ingredients of good report writing.

●   *Beginning*: covers the Introduction but acts as a summary of the whole report.

- *Middle*: covers Image, Production Plans, Specification and Engine Details.
- *End*: contains the Conclusion and Recommendation.

Applying the same criteria:

1. Does this report flow, and is the content easy to follow and understand?
2. Are there a sufficient number of headings?
3. Are the sentences short and understandable?
4. Does it avoid jargon (technical language that is not clear to the lay person), factual errors, apparent inconsistencies and contradictions?
5. Has the writer expressed him/herself clearly and kept the reader's interest?

Again, the answer is 'yes' every time.

"I only volunteered!"
Most people find that, once they have joined a voluntary organisation, sooner or later they are asked to write a report! This may simply involve making a modest contribution to the local Parish Magazine, the Church Yearbook, or a local charity newsletter. This is not as daunting a task as you may imagine.

Consider the following example, taken from a Parish Magazine, which was contributed by the Secretary of the Women's Institute titled (a little unimaginatively) *Women's Institute*:

In June the Women's Institute had their 'Members Own' competition, where members each enter three items of their choice for judging. Eleven members took part and we had an excellent display of Craft and Cookery, including toys, padded picture frames, embroidered pictures, calendars, cushions, pies, cakes, preserves and flower arrangements.

Mrs Margaret . . . was judge and she had a difficult task. The winners were:

1st Mrs Joy . . .
2nd Mrs Renate . . .
3rd Mrs Betty . . .

> **Craft Cup** Mrs Joy . . .
> **Cookery Cup** Mrs Renate . . .
> Thank you to all members who entered and made such a good show. Our President, Mrs Frances . . ., gave a report of her trip to Birmingham for the Triennial General Meeting of Nationwide Women's Institutes.

Applying the criteria we examined in the first chapter when we identified the main characteristics of a report, this short, simple report:

- *Has a clear purpose.*
- *Is organised systematically.*
- *Targets a specific audience.*

It appears in the Parish Magazine, a local publication of general interest, and is aimed at those readers who took part in the 'Members Own' competition. However, it has limited interest to the majority of readers.

- *The introduction* explains the background to the competition and the range of entries received.
- *The main report* gives the results of the competition.
- *The conclusion* explains the contribution the President made to the meeting.

The style of this report could be improved. It does not flow particularly well and the conclusion is not linked clearly to the competition results. However, it demonstrates how easily a simple report can be written.

The next example is a report found in a Church Magazine titled *Local Church Agapé*. The report does not explain that an 'agapé' is a love feast of the early Christians at Communion time, but presumes the readers are well informed.

> The local churches' agapé will take place on Tuesday 3rd August at 7.30pm in the hall of the United Reform Church. The theme this year will be 'The Wisdom and Power of God'. A LOVE with a difference equals a GOD LIKE LOVE, that is AGAPÉ?

Without God's Wisdom and Power, could we have reached our 8th agapé?

An opportunity will be given to members from each church to take part; hymns, Bible and other readings will be used. There will be a SHARED SUPPER around the table, when members can offer their own thoughts, prayers, or a favourite hymn. A time of silence will end this year's supper.

If you still have your tree from last year please bring it along.

A warm welcome to everyone.

This report has a clear purpose – to inform everyone about the agapé supper – but it has several weaknesses in its structure and digresses in the middle to ask its readers a rhetorical question.

Towards the end of the piece the writer inexplicably reminds readers to bring their tree along. The reasons for this are not clear to the general reader, nor to anyone unfamiliar with practice in previous years.

Finally, the use of capital letters to add emphasis is inappropriate and distracting.

In terms of meeting the criteria of 'understanding the reader's needs' it has several shortcomings, and fails these tests:

- *Is it user friendly?*
- *Is the meaning clear?*
- *Is it easily understood?*
- *Is the style natural?*

5

THE METHODICAL APPROACH

You need a methodical approach, otherwise you will waste time.
So, before starting:

- be clear what information you need
- decide whom to consult
- establish your research material.

To fail to prepare is to prepare to fail. Preparation time is
essential, otherwise you miss out important points (and discover
half way through writing the report that you need to start afresh).
The time is amply repaid when you produce a document which
flows smoothly and does not ramble.

The *METHOD* that follows is designed to be easy to remember
and encourage a self disciplined approach:

- *M*ind-mapping
- *E*diting
- *T*idying up the loose ends
- *H*aving a plan
- *O*rganising the material
- *D*elivering the finished report.

Mind-mapping

Jot down on paper all your thoughts on the subject, emulating the
technique of brain-storming. Let one idea trigger off another
related idea, and another, and more and more!

List all the interrelated ideas shown below, then join with a
line those that interconnect.

Example 1

DEER CONTROL

Past		Old
	Methods of control	Devon & Somerset pack
Present		Weak
	Wolves	Quantock pack
Future		Lame
	Hounds	Tiverton pack
		Injured
	Shooting	New Forest Buckhounds
West Country	Hunting	
	National picture	Shooting
150 hunted		7 hour chase
	80,000 killed	Efficient
1,000 culled		25 mile chase
	99% shot	Humane
Red Deer		Selective
		male fallow
hinds		1st Aug-31st Oct
		stags
bucks		1st Nov-28th Feb
		Spring stags
roe bucks		1st Mar-30th Apr

Example 2

DEER CONTROL

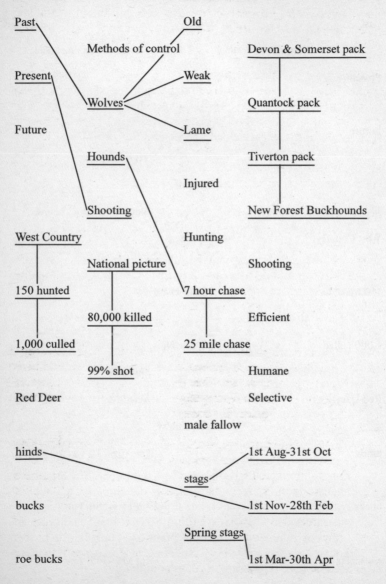

Past

Old

Methods of control

Devon & Somerset pack

Present

Weak

Wolves

Quantock pack

Future

Lame

Hounds

Injured

Tiverton pack

Shooting

Hunting

New Forest Buckhounds

West Country

National picture

Shooting

150 hunted

7 hour chase

80,000 killed

Efficient

1,000 culled

25 mile chase

99% shot

Humane

Red Deer

Selective

male fallow

hinds

1st Aug-31st Oct

stags

bucks

1st Nov-28th Feb

Spring stags

roe bucks

1st Mar-30th Apr

Editing
This is the stage when you rearrange the material and select what you wish to use in the final report. Some useful facts and ideas may have to be left out because they are peripheral. Rank the material available in order of priority, including only what is most important and relevant.

Tidying up the Loose Ends
There may be additional arguments and statistics which are particularly compelling. Decide where they best fit in. The objective should be to develop and amplify certain aspects of the text, giving it greater depth and authority.

Consider including illustrations, and whether charts or graphs are necessary and would add impact. Example three (overleaf) shows the factual information at this stage.

Have a Plan
This is where you consider how to present the material to have maximum impact. It must now be organised into a logical sequence with a beginning which introduces the subject, a middle to develop the main theme and arguments, followed by the end which draws the report to a logical conclusion.

In this report the plan is as follows:

- *Beginning*
  This introduces the reader to the subject of deer hunting. It provides background information about the packs of hounds which operate in the West Country and New Forest and how they systematically target stags, hinds, Spring stags and bucks at particular times of the year.
- *Middle*
  This provides a historical perspective and explains how nature regulates the deer population. It contrasts this with the cruelty involved in using hounds to hunt deer. The argument against hunting deer with hounds is developed. The level of regulation necessary to manage the deer population is considerable. This involves culling 80,000 deer each year in order to maintain a stable population. Deer hunting with hounds is seen as not only cruel but ineffective as it is quite incapable of regulating the deer population.

Example 3

DEER CONTROL

Past	Present	Hounds
Wolves	Shooting	7 hour chase
Old		25 mile chase
Weak		
Lame		

West Country	National picture
150 hunted	80,000 killed
1000 culled	99% shot

Hinds	Stags	Spring stags
1st Nov-28th Feb	1st Aug-31st Oct	1st Mar-30th Apr

Devon & Somerset pack
Quantock pack
Tiverton pack
New Forest Buckhounds

Additional facts to include:
a)   In the New Forest the bucks are hunted during September, and from 1st November until 30th April.
b)   Roe bucks have been hunted in the South West since 1989.
c)   The Exmoor and Quantock herd totals 7-8,000 deer and requires an annual cull of over 1,000 deer to maintain a stable population.
d)   Controlled shooting is necessary to maintain the correct sex ratio.
e)   Shooting is carried out by professional marksmen using a high-powered rifle with telescopic sights.
f)   Deer can be culled humanely and efficiently by shooting.

- *End*

   The conclusion demonstrates that a carefully controlled shooting programme can control the population effectively and humanely.

Organise the Material

This means rearranging the material you have chosen to use in the final report in a way that is consistent with the 'plan' you have devised. Using the material contained in the previous example and the outline plan, results in example 4.

Example 4

- *Beginning*

Packs in the West Country:	Devon and Somerset
	Quantock
	Tiverton
Packs in the South:	New Forest Buckhounds

Stags hunted 1st August-31st October.
Hinds hunted 1st November-28th February.
Spring stags hunted 1st March-30th April.
Bucks hunted in September and from 1st November-30th April.
New packs hunting roe bucks in the South West since 1989.

- *Middle*

Wolves in the past killed the weak, lame and old.
Hounds exhaust the victims with a 7 hour chase over 25 miles.
In the West Country, hunting kills only 150 deer yet 1000 deer need to be culled each year.
Annually 80,000 need to be culled, of which 99% are shot.

- *End*

Controlled shooting is necessary to maintain the correct sex ratio and maintain a stable population.
Shooting is carried out by professional marksmen.
Deer can be culled humanely and efficiently by shooting.

Delivering the Finished Report

Now all that remains is to select a suitable title, incorporate some headings into the text and write the first draft.

The best method is to compose the first draft on a word processor or computer. This allows you to rearrange sentences, tidy up the grammar and check the spelling as you go along.

Always use double spacing, then you will have sufficient room to correct errors and make minor alterations to the text manually.

Dictating a report to a secretary, or into a Dictaphone, requires skill and practice. You may prefer to write the report out in longhand and, once satisfied, arrange to have it typed. Provided you leave yourself plenty of space to incorporate alterations, this method works well. However, if you decide to make major alterations, or changes in the order or construction of paragraphs, you may need to rewrite the draft completely, which is time-consuming.

The more time you spent in preparation and organising your material, the easier this stage of compiling the final report is.

Be self-critical as you review your grammar, sentence construction, spelling and punctuation. Aim for clarity. This is a priority in a professional report.

Once the first draft is complete and typed you should read it through carefully and check it for errors. Some writers prefer to read their reports out aloud, as poor grammar and overlong sentences stand out more readily. If you have a colleague or critical friend who is willing to check it over, so much the better. Another pair of eyes can prove invaluable.

Once you are satisfied the report is clear, accurate and readable, it can be typed, or finalised on the computer. You should double check it for any new errors that may have crept in, then submit it to the manager who requested it, ensuring that it is received on time.

Example 5 shows the completed report. This extract from *Deer and Staghunting* is reproduced with kind permission from the League Against Cruel Sports.

Example 5

DEER HUNTING AND DEER CONTROL

Introduction
Red Deer are hunted by three packs of hounds in the West Country – the Devon and Somerset, Quantock and Tiverton

Staghounds – and in the south the New Forest Buckhounds hunt male fallow deer.

Deer Hunting
The three West Country packs hunt Autumn stags (mature males) from 1st August-31st October, the hinds (females) from 1st November to the end of February, and Spring stags (young males) from the start of March to the end of April. In the New Forest, the bucks are hunted in September and from the end of April. Since 1989, new packs have been formed to hunt roe bucks in the South West.

Deer Control
In the past, wild predators such as wolves would have selected the old, weak or lame deer, the object being a short chase and a quick kill. Conversely, the object of deer hunting with hounds is to provide a long chase for the hunt followers. Exhausting the victim over a seven hour, twenty-five mile chase is clearly inefficient.

The West Country deer hunt kills approximately 150 deer a year, yet the Exmoor and Quantocks herds of 7-8,000 would require an annual cull in excess of 1,000 to maintain a stable population. Nationally each year at least 80,000 deer are killed by shooting. This is the method usually employed and accounts for 99% of the annual cull.

Conclusion
Carefully controlled shooting will remove the old and sick deer, and is necessary to maintain the correct sex ratio to avoid over-population. A skilled professional marksman using a high-powered rifle fitted with telescopic sights will kill a grazing deer instantly, humanely and efficiently.

6

DEVELOPING A PERSONAL STYLE

Making a Positive Impact

Style and structure are the two factors that most affect impact.

Style describes the way words are selected and put together into sentences. Developing a readable style is the way to make a positive impact. It demands an appreciation of syntax and the rules of grammar, especially:

- how paragraphs are shaped
- how sentences are constructed
- the choice of vocabulary
- how to form phrases and clauses
- how to punctuate
- how best to illustrate and use diagrams
- how to lay out your writing.

The relationship between writer and reader is a delicate one. You need quickly to establish a rapport with the reader, to find common ground based on shared values, similar attitudes and experiences, and an outlook that is complementary.

The method used to create this rapport is called style. The skill is to adapt your writing style to match the expectations and requirements of your readers. Some of the considerations that will affect your choice of style are as follows:

- *Age*
  The young appreciate a different approach from the elderly.

- *Education and level of intelligence*
  Pitch the complexity of your language and the breadth of your vocabulary at levels appropriate to your readers.
- *Background and experience*
  Your readers may be professional people, technical experts, work colleagues, political figures and those with a classical or literary background. On the other hand they may be ordinary lay people with an interest in the subject.
- *Outlook and attitudes*
  Look for shared values, personal preferences, interests, prejudices, differences in social class and culture.

The style adopted in Example 1 is geared for children under ten years old. Notice how the writer adopts a personal, conversational style and uses a limited vocabulary. This piece uses good grammar but is in keeping with the reader's age and experience of life.

Example 1

Do you like exploring? My brother enjoys climbing very much. He climbs over fences, climbs up trees, clambers into ditches and over stiles. My mother used to worry about him and say, "One day John will fall down and break an arm or a leg."

My Dad used to say to her, "Don't worry, he's a boy. Boys will be boys. If he is careful he will be all right."

One day my brother decided to try and climb onto the front gate. He climbed up carefully and managed to balance himself astride the gate. He could see all the people going up and down the road. He thought he was very clever and grown up. He called out, "Hello Mrs Jones, hello Mrs Blake" as they passed by. They were surprised to see him perched on top of the gate. "Please be careful, John, or you will fall off and hurt yourself." "Don't worry, I'm all right. I'm grown up now."

Example 2 is aimed at the young teenager and seeks to adopt the street language of teenagers. It adopts a personal style and tries to be familiar and establish rapport by adopting a chatty and matey approach. This style is common in teenage magazines which are trying hard to hold the reader's attention. It breaks many of the conventional rules by adopting slang and deliberately using poor grammar, because the writers know teenagers have a limited attention span. They tailor their style to what they believe has street cred(ibility).

Example 2

ALL YOU NEED TO KNOW ABOUT KISSING!

Loads of girls think you've got to like kissing by a certain age, and so they pretend to fancy lads and get into kissing because they think their mates will laugh at them if they make out they are not interested yet. A lot of girls think that as soon as they go out with a lad they should prove they like them by kissing them on the first date.

Kissing should never be something you do because you think you are expected to, there is no timetable for kissing and you should not rush things. There is nothing wrong with not wanting to get into a snogging session with your boyfriend. There is no point in kissing someone so that you can be like all your mates. If you are too keen to start kissing him, he may think you want to go further. The way to avoid any confusion with a fella is to get to know him first by talking to him. It may be embarrassing talking about snogging and what you want out of the relationship, but it's much better to let a lad know where he stands, than to have him wondering what is going on.

Example 3 is aimed at women of all ages, but particularly those in their thirties. It treats the reader as an intelligent equal, who has plenty of life experience, but is seeking information in order to pursue a healthy lifestyle. The writer adopts a style which establishes a good rapport and appeals to a set of common values and social attitudes. Any hint of a patronising tone is carefully avoided.

Example 3

HEALTHY EATING TIPS

Here are four great reasons for eating bread: it could help you live longer; you'll look better; it relieves the symptoms of premenstrual tension; it will invigorate you.

In Great Britain we all eat too much fat and not enough vitamins, minerals and carbohydrates. As a result we risk cancer, coronary disease and strokes. All bread provides protein, carbohydrates and, most important of all, fibre. The best is wholemeal bread as this has the most fibre. Bread also contains niacin, a Vitamin B which keeps eyes and skin looking healthy and bright.

In a recent study, nearly two-thirds of women who changed their diet to include more bread and starchy foods found they experienced relief from PMT symptoms.

Further research has revealed that a breakfast rich in carbohydrates, which provide the body with the hydrogen and oxygen it needs, can positively improve your mood. This is because they give your body the boost it needs first thing in the day. If you want to be more alert, perk up yourself with a slice of bread. Over one-third of the thiamine you need, a Vitamin B1, comes from products like bread or cereal.

Example 4 is aimed at a reader who is well-informed about matters of current interest in the world of science. The style used is measured, the language balanced, and the appeal is to an intelligent, well-educated, middle class audience.

Example 4

The UFO conspiracy theorists will not be surprised to learn that evidence exists to support the widely held view that an extraterrestrial object crashed in 'Area 51' in Nevada, USA. The UFO theorists believe that Area 51 is the nerve centre for research on aliens being conducted by the USA military. This belief is widely held inasmuch as the residents of the nearby town, Rachel, have named a local road 'Extraterrestrial Highway'.

A geographical survey has discovered evidence that the alien invader was in fact a comet with a diameter of four miles which hit the earth 370 million years ago. The evidence proves that Area 51 lies in a comet impact zone because the area is rich in the metal iridium and grains of shocked quartz have been discovered. Both of these geographical features are only produced when major impacts by comets occur.

Example 5 is from a report aimed at a professional audience who are studying world religions. The writer concentrates on being factual and objective. The style adopted is passive and impersonal. This approach may appeal to a wider audience because it is written in non-technical language, and can be appreciated by a lay person.

Example 5

Christians believe that God created heaven and earth, and that he sent his son Jesus Christ into the world. Mary, a virgin, gave birth to Jesus who was conceived by the Holy Spirit. He was crucified, died and resurrected on the third day, and later ascended to heaven where he will remain until he returns to judge the living and the dead. After the Ascension Christians received the power of the Holy Spirit and the church was born and developed worldwide. Christians believe in the Holy Spirit, the Holy Catholic Church, the forgiveness of sins, the resurrection of the body, and in everlasting life.

Over the centuries the church has divided into many denominations and includes the Roman Catholic Church, the Church of England, and the Free Churches, which includes Baptists, Methodists, Pentecostals, Quakers, the Salvation Army and the United Reformed churches.

The weekly celebration of the resurrection takes place on a Sunday when the Holy Eucharist, Holy Mass, Holy Communion or the Lord's Supper are celebrated. Services are also held on Christmas Day, Good Friday and Easter

Day. Ash Wednesday is celebrated as a Holy Day by Roman Catholics.

Christians believe that the writers of the Bible were inspired by God and treat it as sacred. The Old Testament contains 39 Jewish Scriptures and the New Testament contains 27 books. These include the Gospels, about the life of Jesus, the Acts of the Apostles, about the early church, and Christian teaching and prophecy.

There is no special diet for Christians, although some Christians fast during Lent and Roman Catholics fast on Ash Wednesday and Good Friday.

Only Christian clergy and lay people participating in services wear any special clothing. Many Christians wear a cross, crucifix or use rosary beads.

Getting the Tone Right

Is there a formal relationship with the reader, as exists when you are writing for:

- managers in the hierarchy within the same organisation
- collateral colleagues
- subordinates in the same section or office?

There is a wide range of formal communications:

- reports to committees, senior managers and the Board of Directors
- reports for publication which arouse public interest and media attention.
- confidential reports to a lawyer, the courts, a tribunal or disciplinary hearing
- reports for clients and external customers
- inter-departmental announcements or returns which have limited general interest or commercial significance
- routine internal communications.

Formal communications are often sent to people who do not know you, so they are entirely reliant on the quality of your writing to convey the meaning clearly. A well laid out report which uses Standard English, is grammatically correct, and adopts the right *tone*, is a successful one.

Tone, therefore, describes the way the chosen words are expressed, and the feelings they invoke in the reader. Tone is an important element of the way you communicate your attitudes about the subject matter to the intended readership.

Vocabulary is another conveyor of tone. Language can be either formal, as in a report to your manager; or informal, as when writing for a teenage audience. Having decided on an appropriate style, be consistent throughout the report. Unless, of course, you want to change style deliberately to achieve a particular effect!

Consider the following references to a male person and the police:

| a) young man | boy | lad | fella |
| b) police officer | policeman | copper | fuzz |

Example 1
The following language is used on a formal occasion:

1a) young man   1b) police officer

Example 2
Standard English is what the majority of people use in common speech:

2a) boy   2b) policeman

Example 3
Colloquial language is what most people would use in every-day speech. It is familiar language which might be used in dialogue, but would not be used in a formal report, letter or memorandum:

3a) lad   3b) copper

Example 4
Slang is street language or jargon characteristic of a particular social class, such as cockney rhyming slang. Sometimes it is used

in a disrespectful way but more often slang is incomprehensible to those 'not in the know'. Consider the following examples:

4a) fella   4b) fuzz

7

MASTERING THE BASIC TECHNIQUES

Using Paragraphs Correctly

Large amounts of unbroken prose make for heavy reading. Break up a page into several paragraphs to make it more digestible. A report generally features shorter paragraphs than an article or book, because most reports are fact intensive and difficult to absorb if served up in unpalatable chunks.

A paragraph may contain only a single sentence. Usually it comprises a number of sentences which share a common theme and are linked together in a logical manner. A paragraph introduces one idea at a time which may be developed in subsequent paragraphs. Do not include a different subject in the same paragraph.

A complete report has a clear structure: a beginning, a middle and an end. The structure of a paragraph mirrors this formula in miniature.

Every paragraph has one main point to communicate. This is expressed in a variety of ways depending on the impact the writer intends.

In the first example the most important point is contained in the opening sentence. This key sentence is supported by subsequent sentences which expand on the theme, and provide further information, examples or explanation to support the text.

Example 1

HELPING YOUR BOSS TO BUILD THE BUSINESS

You will not gain the confidence of your boss and help him make the business profitable unless he is convinced he can rely on your unswerving support. There is more to this than convincing him that you do your job well. He is looking for someone he can trust and who is able to complement areas where he has weaknesses. The way forward is to demonstrate you are indispensable, that you are loyal, supportive (but not a 'yes' man), and a team member.

The opening sentence makes a clear and emphatic statement about the importance of gaining your boss's confidence. How this can be achieved is explained in the sentences that follow, which outline the personal and professional attributes necessary to achieve this goal.

In the second example the key sentence occurs in the middle of the paragraph. This allows the writer to build up the reader's interest, make the key point, then explain or develop the idea in subsequent sentences.

Example 2

DEVELOPING COMPETITIVE STRATEGIES AND
MANAGING CHANGE

The world of commerce and marketing does not stand still. The ability of a business to embrace change is key to its survival. *A business needs a flexible organisation and an enlightened management in tune with the realities of the changing market place.* Only then can management motivate and enthuse its staff to face new challenges like launching new products.

In this final example the main point is deliberately held back to the end while the reader's interest is steadily built up. It becomes the climax of the paragraph in order to achieve maximum impact.

Example 3

WORKING FOR A WINNER

Everyone wants to be part of a winning team where enthusiasm, motivation, self belief is high, and team members are keen to support and co-operate with each other. Leaders of winning teams make sure efforts are channelled profitably into maximising output and achieving high standards. With your boss do you have evidence of the following skills?

a)   They are a good communicator with well developed listening skills, receptive to new ideas, and an innovator.

b)   They are supportive and stimulate the team to achieve their targets.

c)   They display a high level of concern for the welfare of the team.

d)   They have high standards and expectations of the team, but have an enviable knowledge base, and challenge the team to be the best.

e)   They are willing to delegate.

f)   They adopt a participative style of management, treating you as an equal.

g)   They are appreciative of your best efforts and give honest, constructive feedback.

If your boss measures up to this specification, then you are working for a winner!

The structure of this paragraph makes the reader absorb all the preceding sentences before releasing the punch-line which is saved for the final sentence and is contained in the final word, thus ending the paragraph on a high note.

Constructing Sentences

Your report may be the only contact you have with your audience. So use language effectively and develop your technical skills.

Badly constructed sentences which are disjointed and ramble

will create a poor impression. The use of slang, clichés or jargon must be avoided. Spelling mistakes and poor punctuation are sloppy and unprofessional, which may have far reaching consequences.

A carefully written sales proposal or well researched report may bring in thousands of pounds worth of business. It could determine that your advice and recommendations are translated into action. It may enhance your professional reputation.

A badly produced document will lose the order, be ignored by people who matter, or undermine your credibility.

Here are five rules for you:

1. *understand basic grammar*
2. *understand syntax*
3. *spell correctly*
4. *avoid the common errors*
5. *punctuate correctly.*

Understand Basic Grammar
Every sentence must contain a noun (or pronoun) and a verb. A noun is a naming word and can be either concrete or abstract. A concrete noun may be a person, place or thing. Abstract nouns may express thoughts, feelings and ideas.

Nouns
Consider the following sentences which identify nouns:

a) *Janet* [noun] travelled all the way to *London* [noun].
b) The *office* [noun] was situated in the middle of town.

Pronouns
Pronouns are words that can replace a noun in a sentence. In the case of people, the name would be replaced by I, mine, you, he, she, her, him, we, us, they, them or their. The following sentences contain pronouns:

a) *She* [pronoun] travelled all the way to London [noun].
b) Janet [noun] went to the office in town. At five o'clock *she* [pronoun] came home.

Verbs

A verb is a doing word and represents some kind of action, a thought process, a state or a condition. The following words are verbs: carry, walk, think, drive. In the following sentences the verbs are in italics:

a)   Always *carry* [verb] a fire extinguisher in your car [noun].
b)   John [noun] must *think* [verb] out a solution to the problem.
c)   They [pronoun] *walked* [verb] to the office from all over town.

Adverbs

An adverb is used to extend the meaning of a verb or, funnily enough, an adjective. This takes the form of additional information to supplement that provided by the verb or adjective, like how, when, where, how many. Most adverbs can be identified by their *'ly'* endings. The following examples show this quite clearly:

a)   John [noun] sat down *quietly* [adverb] to think out a solution.
b)   The lawn was *mainly* [adverb] green [adjective] but *partly* [adverb] brown [adjective].

Adjectives

Adjectives are descriptive words and provide further information about a noun. Examples of adjectives are words like: large, bright, beautiful, rusty. Adjectives normally precede the noun or pronoun they qualify, or follow the verb 'to be'. In the following examples the adjectives are in italics:

a)   A *rusty* [adjective] fire extinguisher may fail.
b)   John [noun] is *strong* [adjective] and *muscular* [adjective] after doing weight training.

Prepositions

These are words used immediately before a noun or pronoun, to show how it relates to another person or object referred to in the sentence.

a) John's [noun] car was much bigger *than* [preposition] the car owned by Jane [noun].

b) Jane [noun] knew her car was very different *from* [preposition] the car owned by John [noun].

c) Is Paul [noun] subject *to* [preposition] a profit sharing scheme?

d) The boss [noun] is accountable and answerable *for* [preposition] your [pronoun] work, your [pronoun] mistakes, your [pronoun] failures.

Conjunctions

A conjunction is a linking word used to join ideas together by acting as a bridge between words, phrases or sentences. Among conjunctions used to introduce independent ideas are: when, where, because, whether, in order that, after, unless, as soon as. Some conjunctions are used in pairs like: 'not only/but also' and 'either/or'.

Common examples are words like 'and', 'but' and 'or' which arise in the following two sentences:

a) The fire extinguisher was very rusty. It worked satisfactorily.

   The word 'it' is replaced by the preposition 'but' which allows the sentences to be joined together.

   The fire extinguisher was very rusty *but* [preposition] worked satisfactorily.

b) Is he an adversarial boss who enjoys conflict? Does he avoid difficult issues that will upset people?

   These two sentences could be joined together by using the word 'and'. However, 'or', which is also a preposition, is the more appropriate here.

   Is he an adversarial boss who enjoys conflict *or* [preposition] does he avoid difficult issues that will upset people?

Interjection

The interjection is used most frequently in direct speech and conveys a sense of emotion. Words like Ouch! Oh! Ah! and What! are exclamations and are often followed by an exclamation mark.

a)   Ouch! That hurt.
b)   Ah, I can see more clearly now.

Understand Syntax
Syntax is the grammatical structure of sentences.

A sentence is a grouping of two or more words which conveys a single thought. Sentences may be short, and convey an idea contained in a single clause. These are called simple sentences. Longer sentences which contain several clauses, and may deal with a number of complex pieces of information, are known as major sentences. Syntax is closely linked to style. It is the way in which you create word groupings to develop your ideas, and convey your meaning, through words, phrases, clauses and sentences.

A phrase is a group of words without a verb which is used to add meaning to nouns or verbs.

A clause is a short sentence which is linked to another by a conjunction to form a lengthier and more complex sentence. These linked clauses will contain several ideas within the form of a single sentence.

The impact of your writing is determined by the syntax (how words are joined together) and your choice of vocabulary (the words chosen to convey meaning).

There are several ways that sentences are constructed:

- *Statements*. Most sentences are statements. Consider the following: At five o'clock Mr Jones leaves the office and goes home.
- *Commands*. A command is an instruction or order: Leave the office and go home.
- *Exclamations*. An outcry or yell which is abrupt and to the point: Go home!
- *Questions*. A question asks or enquires about someone or something and requires a response. A rhetorical question is asked purely for effect and does not expect to be answered: Are you going home at five o'clock?
  Who would have thought it? [rhetorical]

The tone of your writing should be consistent with the type of report you are writing. Most reports are written in a personal, active voice:

a)   I would like you to consider the following recommendations.

b)   I have decided to consult the staff about your recommendations.

Some investigative writing, reports to committees, or technical submissions, require that an impersonal tone is adopted. This means that 'you' and 'I' are kept out of the text and the third person – 'he', 'she', 'it', 'they' – is used instead:
It was decided to make the following recommendations.

Using the passive form of the verb has a similar effect: 'I have decided to consult the staff about your recommendations' becomes:
The staff will be consulted about your recommendations.

This leaves out the phrase 'by me' which is implicit, and alters the tone, making it impersonal.

Sentences must be Complete
The test is to check that every sentence contains a noun (the subject) and a verb (the doing word).

Select words that are active and expressive to convey your meaning in a more interesting way. Use short sentences for greater dramatic impact. Avoid making all sentences the same length. Vary the length so as to inject pace into your writing and build steadily towards the climax. When you finally deliver your punch line it will have maximum effect.

It is good practice to intersperse long and short sentences to vary the pace and maintain interest. Do not, however, construct sentences that are *too* complex and involved. The maximum length of any sentence should be twenty words, particularly if they are multisyllabic. Otherwise you risk becoming longwinded, and will not hold your reader's attention.

Spell Correctly
Spelling mistakes can easily be avoided by purchasing a good dictionary and using the spellcheck on your computer or word processor. However, there are some words which are particularly problematic and no spellcheck will be able to help you with

homophones. These are words that sound alike but have different meanings.

There are a number of rules, and several guidelines, which if followed will help you avoid most problematic areas.

Absolute rule
'q' is always followed by 'u'.

Homophones
These words sound the same but have different meanings, eg:
    stationery (writing materials) and stationary (not moving)
    air (the earth's atmosphere) and heir (one who inherits)
    coarse (rough) and course (meal portion or race track)
    what (how much) and watt (a unit of electricity).

Prefixes
The most important thing to remember is that adding a prefix to a word does not alter the basic spelling. Consider the following words: appear becomes *disappear* or *reappear*
    necessary becomes *unnecessary*
    active becomes *proactive, inactive* or *reactive.*
    In a few instances, prefixes are added to a word by means of a hyphen, like *pre-emptive, co-operative.*

Suffixes
Adding 'ly' is straight forward even for words that end in an 'l':
    free becomes *freely*
    love becomes *lovely*
    critical becomes *critically*
    convincing becomes *convincingly.*

Plurals
In general, adding an 's' to the singular form makes the plural in the majority of cases: budgie becomes *budgies*
    girl becomes *girls.*

However, the following exceptions apply:

a)   Nouns ending in 'ch', 'x', 'sh' or 'ss' form the plural by adding 'es' as the following examples show:

lurch becomes *lurches*
box becomes *boxes*
fish becomes *fishes*
mass becomes *masses*.

b) Some nouns ending in 'f' or 'fe' change to 'ves' in the plural:
    calf becomes *calves*
    thief becomes *thieves*.
  Others like hoof become *hooves* but can also be spelt hoofs.
  Words like staff become *staves* meaning 'a strong stick'.
  Alternatively, staff can become *staffs* if you mean a 'bodies of officers'.

c) Nouns ending in 'y' which are preceded by a consonant take the ending 'ies' in the plural:
    spy becomes *spies*
    lady becomes *ladies*
    authority becomes *authorities*.

d) Some words remain the same in the plural as in the singular form, for instance: *sheep, deer* and *salmon*.

General guidelines
a) The accepted wisdom is 'i' comes before 'e' except after 'c' when the sound made is 'ee':
    believe
    achieve
    shield
    conceive
    receive
    ceiling
  However, there are exceptions to this guideline, such as 'seize' and 'counterfeit'.

b) Words ending in a single 'l' which contain a vowel immediately before them are doubled before a suffix is added:
    crystal becomes *crystallise*
    actual becomes *actually*
    typical becomes *typically*
    real becomes really

Problem Words

Some words are commonly misspelled and cause many people problems. The following words are ones in which mistakes are frequently made. The part of the word which causes difficulty has been highlighted; you need to learn the correct spelling in each case. (In American English, some words may be spelt differently.)

accessible	accessory	accidentally
accommodation	acquaintance	acquire
aggressive	analysis	appalling
argument	assassin	awkward
bachelor	bailiff	behaviour
beneficial	benefited	bicycle
cannibal	capital	catarrh
caterpillar	cellular	changeable
chargeable	commemorate	committed
committee	conscience	contemptible
deferment	deferred	democracy
develop	development	different
disappear	discreet	dissatisfy
disseminate		
ecstasy	eczema	embarrass
endeavour	equipped	exceed
exhilarating	extreme	except
favourite	February	fervour
fictitious	forfeit	fulfil

gauge

gnat

grateful

glamour

government

grievous

glamorous

grammar

guide

handkerchief

honorary

harass

humorous

hindrance

hypocrisy

illegible

intelligible

invigorate

immovable

intriguing

irrelevant

independence

invalidity

irresponsible

jewellery

justification

juvenile

kangaroo

kayak

khaki

laboratory

lightning

leisure

liquor

lieutenant

litre

maintenance

miniature

manoeuvre

miscellaneous

mattress

mischievous

necessary

neighbour

negligence

neither

negotiation

ninetieth

occasion

occurrence

orthodox

parallel

pigeon

privilege

peripatetic

precede

proceed

peripheral

prejudice

proprietor

quarrelsome

quiescent

quotient

rarefy

regrettable

resistant

rhyme	rigour	ruinous
satellite	scrutinise	sheriff
silhouette	skilful	sphere
spicy	succeed	success
symmetry	sympathy	synonymous
technicality	terrible	tragedy
tuition	turmoil	twelfth
ulterior	unnecessary	unequivocal
vaccine	vacuum	vapour
villain	vinyl	voyeur
wilful	wondrous	woollen
wreath	writhe	wrought
yacht	yield	yokel

Errors to Avoid

Blandness

Bland writing is dull and boring. Your writing should hold attention and stimulate interest, as the following example demonstrates:

"An exiting and stylish Polo-based roadster will be the final flourish of Volkswagon's plan to corner the 'lifestyle' market. Aimed at existing open-top favourites, the low-slung two-seater will be a back-to-basics sports car with an emphasis on driving enjoyment and headturning good looks."

This is a considerable improvement on this bland prose:

"Volkswagon have announced plans to introduce a basic

sports car based on the popular Polo range which will be aimed at young affluent people.''

Officespeak
This is pseudo intellectual writing which is bureaucratic and lacks clarity. One effect of 'officespeak' is to distance the reader from the writer.

- 'Please find enclosed for your perusal' should be *'enclosed is'*.
- 'We respectfully acknowledge receipt of' can be shortened to *'thank you for'*.
- 'Thanking you in anticipation of an early reply' can be replaced by *'please reply by next week'*.

Fashionable language
The problem with trying to be trendy and up-to-date is that phrases quickly become dated and meanings change. This can be embarrassing in some instances, as the following example indicates:

He was feeling happy and gay and was looking for a girl friend.

Other words to avoid which can cause misunderstanding are:

- 'cool' meaning 'all right' – its strict definition is moderately cold
- 'chill' meaning 'calm down' – in common usage it is used to refer to an illness or a cold sensation.
- 'wicked' meaning 'very good' – it has a dictionary definition of evil or immoral.

Clichés
Here are just a few of the many which are hackneyed because of overuse, and have therefore little impact.

- 'Sailing close to the wind' meaning taking risks.
- 'Food for thought' meaning something to think about.

- 'Getting your knickers in a twist' meaning losing your sense of proportion.
- 'Putting the cart before the horse' meaning getting your priorities wrong.

Solecisms
These are breaches of syntax.

- 'An amount of people' should be 'a number of people'.
- 'Different to' should be 'different from'.
- 'Like he said' should be 'as he said'.
- 'Who' should be used when it is the subject, and 'whom' when it refers to the object form.
- Double negatives should be avoided as they reverse the meaning and are contradictory. For instance, the song title *I Can't Get No Satisfaction* should either have been *I Can't Get Any Satisfaction* or *I Can Get No Satisfaction*.

Ambiguity
Many statements are open to misunderstanding because they have two meanings. Ambiguity can arise, for example, with:

- *figurative language*, as it can be taken literally
- *because*, inserted after a negative statement
- *only*, unless it is placed next to the word it qualifies
- any adjectival phrase used in such a way that it is not clear to which noun it relates: 'Piano for sale by lady with one leg missing' is an extreme example.

Avoiding the 'Fog Factor'
Whatever you are writing, your purpose is to communicate effectively and clearly.

Judge your writing by the test of 'readability'. The American Robert Gunning devised the term 'Fog Index' to describe writing which makes for heavy reading. He devised a simple method to measure your readability which is as follows, and I recommend it:

- Select a page at random and count the number of words on the page. (If you have a word processor this is easily accomplished using the word count.) Next, divide the number of words by the number of sentences on the page. This will give you the average number of words in each sentence on the page. Make a note of this number.

- Count all the words on the page which contain three syllables or more per 100 words, and make a note of this number. You should ignore any words which are hyphenated (e.g. user-friendly), any capitalised words (e.g. Amsterdam), any composite words (e.g. businesswoman) and any words of three syllables ending in 'es' or 'ed' (e.g. indices or uprooted).

- Add these two numbers together and multiply by 0.4 to find out your readability index. If the result is greater than 12, your writing is becoming difficult to read. If the score is over 16, only a well-educated readership will understand what you have written. Most popular magazines have a reading difficulty rating of between 8 and 10, and the majority of contemporary authors score under 12.

Use Punctuation Correctly

Punctuation can make or mar a report. Incorrect punctuation interrupts flow and can distort meaning. This distracts and irritates the reader.

Lack of punctuation is as common an error as inaccurate punctuation. One way to counter this tendency is to read aloud the piece you have written. Commas will indicate where you should pause for breath, whereas a full stop says "stop and reflect on what you have read".

The following exercise in punctuation invites you to identify where the capital letters, full stops and commas should be placed (to help you, paragraphing and spelling are correct).

Exercise 1

analysing your boss

the quality of the relationship you develop with your boss is of fundamental importance if you are to develop your full potential and discharge your responsibilities effectively like most successful relationships it is necessary consciously to work at managing the relationship as opposed to trying to manage your boss with the aim of ensuring it is mutually beneficial

although most bosses are ordinary reasonable people there are important differences which become significant in the work situation the principal reason for concentrating on this relationship is that they have power over you in your working life they have differing interests and priorities given that they are responsible not only for their own work but for the work of the whole team or business your boss is accountable and answerable for your work your mistakes your failures this responsibility can be onerous and make some bosses more difficult to deal with than others

(See page **86** for the answer.)

Capital Letters
Capital letters are always used:

1.   to commence a sentence
2.   on names of people and places
3.   for titles
4.   for certain abbreviations
5.   for the first person singular, 'I'.

The following examples illustrate the five ways to use capital letters correctly.

Example 1: To commence a sentence.
     a)   What is your name?
     b)   Always be loyal.

Example 2: Names of people and places.
     a)   "My name is John."
     b)   "Where is Mr Smith's office?"
     c)   St Mary's Hospital has a casualty department.
     d)   The local cinema is called the Plaza.

Example 3: For titles.
     a)   The Prime Minister lives at 10 Downing Street.
     b)   Everybody admires Sir John Harvey-Jones.

Example 4: For certain abbreviations.
- a)   Every MP (Member of Parliament) spends most of his time at Westminster.
- b)   The RNIB (Royal National Institute for the Blind) is a registered charity.

Example 5: For the first person singular, 'I'.
I will do whatever I like.

The Full Stop

A full stop is always used at the end of a sentence. It is sometimes used after initials or when an abbreviation is used.

Example 1
- a)   The 'Surrey Alcohol and Drug Advisory Service' becomes known as S.A.D.A.S. (or SADAS).
- b)   The 'Open University' becomes O.U. (or OU).
- c)   Etcetera is shortened to etc.

The modern trend of using open punctuation aims to reduce punctuation to the absolute minimum. This means full stops are omitted between the letters of, and at the end of abbreviations; punctuation is kept to a minimum on business reports and not used on envelopes.

Consider the following examples of addressing a business letter. The first uses open punctuation, the second full punctuation.

Example 2

Mr A C Elliot	Mr. A.C. Elliot,
Director	Director,
Elliot Right Way Books	Elliot Right Way Books,
Kingswood Buildings	Kingswood Buildings,
Lower Kingswood	Lower Kingswood,
Tadworth	Tadworth,
Surrey	Surrey.
KT20 6TD	KT20 6TD

The Comma

A comma is a short pause inserted in a sentence. The following are examples:

Example 1: To separate words in a list.

Do carry a fire extinguisher, a first-aid kit, a V.H.F. radio and flares.

Example 2: To separate a word or phrase at the start of a sentence.

Finally, a summary of our objectives:

Example 3: To introduce dialogue.

George Eliot, the novelist, wrote, ''Animals are such agreeable friends – they ask no questions, they pass no criticisms.''

Example 4: To add something to a sentence, by way of explanation, without changing the overall sense.

The principal requirement is that everyone, including the skipper, wears a life jacket at all times when the boat is under way.

Example 5: To make a sentence easier to read, and provide a pause for breath.

Boating is an idyllic pastime and on a good day it can be considerably enhanced by the company of your nearest and dearest, children and pets.

The Semi-colon

The semi-colon provides for a longer pause than a comma but shorter than a full stop. Its main use is to link statements which are related but where the subject changes, to add emphasis or to highlight a contrast.

Example 1: To link related statements.

It never ceases to surprise me how quickly a suntan, or sunburn, can develop on skin exposed to the sun and wind; children have delicate skin so do remember their sun hats and an appropriate protective sunblock cream.

Example 2: To add emphasis.

"I must ring the police. We've been warned; he is dangerous."

Example 3: To highlight a contrast.

He started walking through the damp, muddy undergrowth; the moon let shafts of light through the trees.

The Colon
A colon is mainly used to introduce a list, as in the following examples. Sometimes a dash follows. Colon-dash (:-) means the same as colon alone.

DO:	DON'T:
prepare thoroughly	panic if things go wrong
explain the safety rules	rely on the weather
wear a life-jacket	forget to say when you
check weather forecasts	expect to be back

Brackets or Parentheses
Brackets come in two forms, they are either round or square (see page **82**). Round brackets are used to enclose words which add extra meaning to a sentence, or when an abbreviation is used for the first time in a passage alongside an explanation of the full meaning. Subsequent use of the abbreviation is clear to the reader.

Example 1: Words which add to the meaning.

Crewsaver produce a good range of dog buoyancy aids in four sizes which are related to the size and weight of the dog; the small size is also suitable for a nautical cat. They are comfortable (but let your dog get used to wearing it before you go boating) with safe fitting straps and incorporate a lifting harness, which acts as an attachment point for a safety line if desired.

Example 2: An abbreviation used for the first time.

Over the next few years Volkswagen (VW) plan to blitz the market with a range of new models. One of the exciting new models under development with VW engineers is the . . . . . .

Square brackets are reserved for dialogue, where they add extra detail which was not actually said.

Example 3: Square brackets add detail.

The salesman, replying to Mr Jones's question, said, "A life-jacket conforming to BS3595 will provide 33lbs of buoyancy [equivalent to 150 Newtons], and is recommended for non-swimmers."

The Hyphen

A hyphen is used when a long word comes at the end of a line and has to be divided. When this occurs the join should take place between syllables. Personally, I find it distracting. It is preferable to rephrase the sentence without changing the meaning.

Some writers tend to 'invent' hyphenated words. This is a mistake, not least because it is hard to remember exactly what you have done and achieve consistency if the word is used again later in the report. It is better to use either one word, or two words, as appropriate, and to use the hyphenated form only if it is given thus in the dictionary (eg pole-axed, pre-empt, co-opt).

Another use for a hyphen is to replace the word 'to', eg: The warehouse is at 35-45 Fellowes Road.

The Dash

The dash can be used as a single or double dash to signify:

single: an explanation will follow, or a fresh thought or idea.

He decided under pressure to agree to their demands but changed his mind after quiet reflection – not surprising under the circumstances.

double: to add emphasis to the text in a similar way to brackets.

"Believe me my young friend, there is nothing – absolutely nothing – half as much worth doing as messing about in boats," wrote Kenneth Grahame in *The Wind in the Willows*.

The Question Mark
Question marks are normally used at the end of a sentence when a question is posed. They can also indicate a query, as in this example: The next meeting will take place at 1430 hours? on Friday 21st June.

The Exclamation Mark
An exclamation mark can replace a full stop and is used to add emphasis, introduce humour or express surprise. This piece of dialogue combines the use of the question mark with an exclamation mark:

Conscience: "It is easy to tell lies, but how do you feel?"
Tom: "Guilty."
Conscience: "You are!"

Quotation Marks
The above shows how quotation marks are used when reporting dialogue. Inverted commas or quotation marks are used as single or double marks according to preference. However, when quotation marks are used within a quotation then different marks should be used.

Example: "The film '101 Dalmations' is available on video," said John Ball.

Apostrophes
Using apostrophes correctly causes more difficulty than any other punctuation mark. There are three main uses for apostrophes:

1.   in names, eg Michael O'Brien
2.   to show where at least one letter is missing, eg I've, there's, we've
3.   to show possession, eg Richard's shop.

Confusion can arise with *it's* and *its*. When it is short for *it is*, it becomes *it's*. However, no apostrophe is used when *its* means 'belonging to', as the following example illustrates.

Example 1: It's and its

   It's a pity that the dog had *its* back to the burglar, so missed the opportunity to chase him.

Use of the apostrophe in the possessive form is also often confusing because the apostrophe will appear in a different position (either before or after the 's') depending on whether the noun is singular or plural.

Example 2: To show possession.

a)   The *dog's* bone was buried in the garden (singular).
b)   The *dogs'* bones are buried in the garden (plural).

But: If the word ends in 's' anyway, but is not plural, then the singular form applies, eg: He lives in St James's Street.
   If the word is a plural form anyway but doesn't end in 's', then, again, the singular form applies, eg: The children's party ends before the women's meeting starts.

The next exercise covers a good cross-section of the punctuation you are likely to find in a report. Paragraphs should be started as indicated; also the spelling in the passage is correct. However, full stops, commas, semi-colons, hyphens, apostrophes and exclamation marks need to be inserted.
   The lack of punctuation makes the report difficult to compre-

hend on first reading. Parts have to be re-read in order to get the proper sense and meaning, which just underlines how important correct punctuation is.

Exercise 2

children afloat to say nothing of the dog

safety rules afloat need to be simple clear and adhered to without exception the principal requirement is to ensure that everyone including the skipper wears a life jacket or buoyancy aid at all times when the boat is under way

children should also wear theirs when the boat is at anchor as this is a time when they become adventurous a safety harness should be fitted where this is practical especially for toddlers who are not yet steady on their feet practise man overboard drills in sheltered waters this can be good fun and can pay dividends in an emergency do not take unnecessary risks though wear those life jackets and have a safety line attached to the boat

at anchor in calm conditions swimmers can safely leave the boat a boarding ladder is essential and should be in place whenever swimmers are in the water if you have an inflatable dinghy on board this can be lowered and attached to the boat with a line for the non swimmers to enjoy this ploy may give the adults chance to eat a meal in relative peace but keep a good watch on the rest of the crew

the choice of a suitable buoyancy device is crucial but it can also be confusing buoyancy devices should conform to the current british standard see page 16 there are four main types of buoyancy device on the market air only life jackets air foam life jackets family buoyancy aids and active buoyancy aids

air only life jackets come in three varieties and provide a minimum of 150n of buoyancy 50 newtons = 11.24lb the oral and manual CO_2 gas versions while appropriate for non swimmers are not considered suitable for children under eight and are more expensive

air foam life jackets contain some inherent buoyancy in the form of foam which is supplemented by an orally filled air chamber two versions are available the traditional which fits over the head and a front opening zipped jacket type

animals are such agreeable friends they ask no questions they pass no criticisms wrote the novelist george eliot whilst this is true I would avoid taking animals other than dogs afloat cats generally do not appreciate sailing dogs on the other hand are sociable animals and will readily adapt to different environments principally because they like being with you

(See below for the answer.)

Exercise Answers

Exercise 1: Answer

Analysing your boss

The quality of the relationship you develop with your boss is of fundamental importance, if you are to develop your full potential and discharge your responsibilities effectively. Like most successful relationships it is necessary consciously to work at managing the relationship, as opposed to trying to manage your boss, with the aim of ensuring it is mutually beneficial.

Although most bosses are ordinary, reasonable people, there are important differences which become significant in the work situation. The principal reason for concentrating on this relationship is that they have power over you in your working life. They have differing interests and priorities, given that they are responsible not only for their own work but the work of the whole team or business. Your boss is accountable and answerable for your work, your mistakes, your failures. This responsibility can be onerous and make some bosses more difficult to deal with than others.

Exercise 2: Answer

Children Afloat to Say Nothing of the Dog!

Safety rules afloat need to be simple, clear and adhered to without exception. The principal requirement is to ensure that everyone, including the skipper, wears a life-jacket or buoyancy aid at all times when the boat is under way.

Children should also wear theirs when the boat is at anchor, as this is a time when they become adventurous. A safety harness should be fitted where this is practical, especially for toddlers who are not yet steady on their feet. Practise man overboard drills in sheltered waters. This can be good fun and can pay dividends in an emergency. Do not take unnecessary risks though; wear those life-jackets and have a safety line attached to the boat.

At anchor, in calm conditions, swimmers can safely leave the boat. A boarding ladder is essential and should be in place whenever swimmers are in the water. If you have an inflatable dinghy on board this can be lowered and attached to the boat with a line for the non-swimmers to enjoy. This ploy may give the adults chance to eat a meal in relative peace but keep a good watch on the rest of the crew.

The choice of a suitable buoyancy device is crucial but it can also be confusing. Buoyancy devices should conform to the current British Standard (see page 16). There are four main types of buoyancy device on the market: air only life-jackets; air/foam life-jackets; family buoyancy aids; and active buoyancy aids.

'Air only' life-jackets come in three varieties and provide a minimum of 150N of buoyancy (50 Newtons = 11.24lb). The oral and manual CO_2 gas versions, while appropriate for non-swimmers, are not considered suitable for children under eight, and are more expensive.

'Air/foam' life-jackets contain some inherent buoyancy in the form of foam which is supplemented by an orally filled air chamber. Two versions are available: the traditional which fits over the head, and a front opening, zipped jacket type.

'Animals are such agreeable friends - they ask no questions, they pass no criticisms' wrote the novelist George Eliot. Whilst this is true I would avoid taking animals other than dogs afloat. Cats generally do not appreciate sailing. Dogs, on the other hand, are sociable animals and will readily adapt to different environments, principally because they like being with you.

Part Three

RESEARCH AND ANALYSIS

8

RESEARCH FROM
EXISTING SOURCES

Desk research is a systematic approach used to collect relevant information which is collated and analysed. It involves examining all relevant published information on the subject, internal or external.

Desk research gives familiarity with the subject. Supplement it with techniques such as interviewing, convening meetings, devising questionnaires and carrying out product trials.

Be clearly focused. Avoid blind alleys. Keep in mind the following questions:

- What are the essential facts I need to uncover?
- How far should I explore the background and historical context?
- What criteria do I use to determine relevance?
- How much detail is required?

Getting Help
Assistants can track down relevant material for you. But take care to avoid misunderstandings. Give them a written brief of your requirements.

Contact the local librarian to locate relevant books. Examine the index and contents to decide which parts of the text are relevant. Next, scan the material quickly for relevance. If suitable, study the relevant sections in more detail, taking notes as appropriate. You could photocopy an important section. Don't waste time laboriously reading everything that could possibly be useful.

Periodicals, magazines and newspapers are useful for up-to-the-minute news, product test reports and financial information. They can keep you appraised of current trends and developments.

Creative Thinking
Develop the ability to think creatively. Logical analysis and reasoning skills are valuable, but keep an open mind. Don't listen selectively to what you want to hear!

Bounce ideas and impressions off others to encourage feedback. This helps maintain a healthy self-critical approach. It also stimulates your own thinking, generating fresh ideas to explore and analyse. Try 'negative brainstorming', a technique that turns a concept on its head, and examines it from the opposite perspective. It can generate original ideas, for instance, by considering ways of how *not* to achieve the goal you wish. Then reverse the ideas and see if any of the suggestions are worthwhile.

Look at a problem from an imaginary perspective. This approach can produce novel solutions. The idea is you transpose yourself and imagine how you would deal with the problem if you were in a different culture or country; or from the perspective of a date in the future, or even based on another planet! It may sound far-fetched, but Einstein reputedly used this technique to make an important discovery.

Sometimes anomalies (which are by-products of the main focus of the research) can lead to a new line of enquiry developing. This may lead to a significant breakthrough. Sir Alexander Fleming discovered penicillin by investigating a by-product of his research: a piece of mould.

Serendipity is the special aptitude of making significant discoveries almost by chance, as happened with the Velcro fastener. This occurred when George de Mestral became fascinated by how burrs became stuck fast to his clothing. By exercising a healthy curiosity and looking at nature's solution to a problem, he developed an application of the principle to everyday life.

Problem solvers are people who have the capacity to think creatively!

Sources of Information
Your terms of reference will affect the approach and level of research that you can realistically achieve in the time allowed.

Identify sources of information and develop an appropriate methodology. Consider all the following ways of gathering information:

- Access the internal information system.
- Approach external sources of information such as libraries, trade and professional associations, and customers or suppliers.
- Conduct questionnaires.
- Carry out interviews with relevant personnel and customers.
- Observe and study.
- Make a case study, and carry out probability sampling.

Using the Library
Every local authority provides a library service which, in the UK, is free of charge. There may be a large central reference library containing a wide range of facilities.

A registered student of a college can use the full range of college library facilities, and there is normally a professional librarian on site. If you have a university in the vicinity, the authorities will often consider granting permission to access their reference facilities, although they are unlikely to allow books to be borrowed unless you are a registered student.

Specialist libraries cater for the technical needs of particular users, like the British Library Science Reference and Information Service, the British Library National Sound Archive and the British Library Reading Room.

There are also Picture Libraries which can provide photographic images on every conceivable subject. For instance, AKG London Ltd has an Arts and History Picture Library with a collection of 100,000 images, and computerised access to a further nine million in the Berlin AKG Library.

Through the public library you can access the following facilities:

- Reference books, encyclopaedias, reports, journals, magazines, directories, indexes, newspapers, cuttings, local council reports, *Which?* reports, and community information.
- A range of fiction and non-fiction books you can borrow,

which includes text books, academic papers, biographies, dictionaries and thesauri.
- Video and audio tapes, compact discs, transparencies, musical scores and plays.
- Information about historical and archaeological artefacts and Art Galleries.
- Computer terminals, including access to the Internet, software packages and CD-ROM.
- Coin or card operated photocopying facilities, including colour.

Libraries can provide access to a vast amount of information, so you need to be precise about identifying your information needs. Otherwise you will become distracted and waste valuable time.

Knowing your way around the classification and cataloguing system of your local library will prove invaluable. Most British libraries use the Dewey Decimal Classification System, invented by the American librarian Melvil Dewey in 1873. The system works by initially dividing broad subject areas into ten categories and allocating a three figure number to each subject, as follows:

General matters	000-099
Philosophy and allied subjects	100-199
Religion	200-299
Social Sciences	300-399
Languages	400-499
Pure Sciences	500-599
Applied Sciences or Technology	600-699
Arts and Recreational Activities	700-799
Literature	800-899
Geography, Biology and History	900-999

Each of these main classes is further sub-divided; so if you take the category Social Sciences (300-399), it is broken down as follows:

Social Sciences	300
Statistics	310
Political Science	320
Economics	330

Law	340
Public Administration	350
Social Services	360
Education	370
Commerce and Communications	380
Customs and Folklore	390

Further sub-divisions are possible and there is a category for each number within the general subject. In the case of Customs and Folklore which is 390, Costumes and Accessories follows on at 391, Etiquette at 395 and Folklore is 398.

Some catalogue numbers can become very long, because they further sub-divide into decimal places. There is a range of books under the heading 'Research', located under 001.4 and this extends to 001.42. Books about Management found under heading 658 extend to three decimal points. The Dewey system is quite sophisticated because it readily adapts to further sub-divisions of a subject area.

Many libraries have introduced computerised systems for cataloguing their books which enables you to discover:

- *The title*, and ascertain whether a specific title is in stock.
- *The author*, and establish if any other books are available by the same author.
- *The subject*, and then check if any other books on the same subject are in stock.

A book search can be conducted by the professional librarian. Alternatively, you can use the on-line computer searching database and, by using your imagination to key in different words, reveal a range of books in print and other sources of information. Any books identified in public libraries throughout the country can be borrowed for a small fee. (This service may be limited as regards lower priced books which are still available in shops.)

In using material for books and other published sources, take care *not* to infringe copyright. The illustrations and words of other writers are protected by copyright (until 70 years after their death), and cannot be reproduced without the consent of the copyright holder.

Acknowledging Other Writers' Work

Report writers acknowledge the work of other contributors in two ways:

- *A reference* which is a footnote or an acknowledgement made when another person's work is quoted directly or paraphrased in your report.
- *A bibliography* is a list of all the books and articles that contain all the listed reference.

References

References are either 'direct quotations' or 'indirect quotations'.

A *direct quotation* should be included in the text with single inverted commas if it is relatively brief. A much longer quotation should be indented and given a paragraph to itself. There is no need to include quotation marks when quoting a lengthy extract, as in the following example.

Once a deer has been killed, members of the hunt eagerly seek trophies from the carcass. Feet and teeth are hacked from the body to be sold or given to supporters. A stag's head is highly prized, but even the feet of an unborn calf are in great demand.

(Deer and Staghunting, League Against Cruel Sports)

An *indirect quotation* is where you rephrase or paraphrase someone else's article or book, but wish to draw attention to the authority of the source you are using. For instance, the first example could be rewritten in the following way:

When the deer is finally killed, the hunt seek souvenirs for themselves and their supporters. This involves cutting off parts of the deer's anatomy and, in the case of a stag, removing the head, according to the League Against Cruel Sports.

The Bibliography

The bibliography contains a list of all the publications you have consulted for information and quotations. Recommended practice varies about the ideal layout for a bibliography. Normally the details given, on a separate line and in alphabetical order, are the author's surname, initials, title of work, publisher and year of publication, as below:

Brown P	The Art of Writing	The Subtle Press	(year)
Cassidy F	Writing Reports	Rainbow Publications	(year)
Morrison A	How to Punctuate Reports	Bright Mark Press Ltd	(year)

Sources are listed within categories, unpublished works like letters, memoranda, internal reports and statistics appear first. These are followed by published sources which are broken down into three main headings:

- books
- articles from professional journals
- newspaper cuttings and extracts from magazines.

Here is an example bibliography, showing these categories.

Bibliography

Books

Collins P	The Stamp Encyclopaedia	Sharp Press Ltd	(year)
Quinn S	Rare Stamps of the World	Parker Books	(year)
Tulley F	A Guide to Stamp Collecting	Charlton Books	(year)

Articles

Billings L	The Subtle Art of Buying Rare Stamps
	The Philatelist (January [year])
Capon P	Collecting European Stamps
	The Stamp Collector (Autumn [year])

Newspapers, etc.

The Times Newspaper (24 October [year])
The Philatelist Society Annual Report (for [year])

Internal and External Sources

Professional and Trade Associations conduct their own product research and market testing, and can provide information and advice on request. Attend trade fairs and exhibitions in order to obtain catalogues and make contacts who may be able to give specialist advice and information.

Professional associations normally publish their own magazines geared to the needs of their members. The Institute of Management, for example, produces a quarterly newsletter which advises members of new and forthcoming books published by the Institute of Management Foundation. They publish digests and information packs on a wide range of subjects, which are available on CD ROM.

A number of commercial companies have developed large databases and have the capacity to provide specialist technical, statistical and financial data.

Consider sources within your own organisation such as:

- reports and memoranda on file
- previous research
- routine statistics and sales figures
- specialist advisers based in Headquarters
- colleagues and specialists from other disciplines
- the company's own library
- information stored on computer databases.

9

QUESTIONNAIRES, SURVEYS AND MEETINGS

Questionnaires are designed to elicit information and record it uniformly. There are three main ways they may be completed:

- by the respondent without outside assistance
- by the respondent in the presence of the interviewer who can provide clarification, assistance and encouragement
- by the interviewer with and for the respondent, interpreting the answers to some extent.

The problem is that people are unreliable when it comes to filling in forms, and very often they can't be bothered to do it accurately. Questionnaires completed unaided are the least accurate and suffer the lowest completion rates, although they are the cheapest.

Questionnaires contain either closed or open questions. A closed question, often called a multiple choice question, is when a limited range of answers is given for the interviewee to select. An open question is where respondents can answer in their own words, briefly or expansively.

Closed questions, whilst posing restrictions on the person being interviewed, allow the researcher to count and evaluate the responses easily. A properly devised questionnaire can be readily analysed by computer, which can save money and be more accurate. Open questions, though avoiding restrictions, create difficulties for the researcher in processing the results in a statistically meaningful way.

Questionnaire Format

In multiple choice questionnaires, offer an even number of answers to discourage people selecting the easy option (the middle answer). Include some check questions, such as on gender and age, so you can satisfy yourself you have obtained a representative sample. Ensure the questions asked are clear, unambiguous and unbiased. Keep the questionnaire short so as not to deter people. Avoid postal questionnaires; the response rate is often less than 10%, meaning that those who respond are statistically unrepresentative. Sometimes, time permitting, a pilot study can be helpful in ironing out any inconsistencies.

Conducting research raises ethical issues. Everyone who agrees to co-operate with a researcher has rights which must be respected and safeguarded, and each researcher has an obligation to keep information completely confidential. Participants should be given assurances that confidentiality and anonymity will be maintained – vital if the information sought is sensitive and potentially embarrassing. Otherwise they are unlikely to speak freely.

The principle of *informed consent*, enshrined in the Nuremberg Code, is used as a guideline by many researchers. This sets out four conditions that individuals taking part should meet:

● mentally competent to make a decision
● volunteers
● fully informed about the nature of the research
● able to make a sensible decision based on the information provided.

You may want to devise your own code of ethics which can be handed to participants.

The Data Protection Act does not apply to manual systems like index cards or questionnaires, but will affect you if you store identifiable information about individuals on a computer or database. In order to comply with this legislation you must register your system and pay the registration fee. You may need to install security devices to your system to protect confidential information from falling into the wrong hands.

Sampling Techniques

You need a representative sample in order to be statistically valid. The sample needs to be large enough, and to be sufficiently similar to the general population for the results to be generalisable. Take care when planning research, as a sample can be representative in one way, but unrepresentative in another.

Therefore the sample must accurately represent diversity in the population, with the correct proportions by gender, age, ethnic origin, social class, income and qualifications.

One problem you must address is deciding whether to select a large representative sample and settle for a small amount of information, or to select a more restricted sample and obtain a great deal of information about each. Cost considerations mean you constantly face the dilemma of choosing between *breadth* and *depth* in your research.

Choosing a Sample

There are five main options, as follows.

Random Sampling

This involves selecting anybody from the target group entirely at random. For example, you may decide to select one person from each group of 100 names on the electoral roll to answer questions.

Systematic Sampling

This method gives everybody an equal chance of being selected and is similar to random sampling. The difference is that it is a systematic approach because every 100th name on the electoral register is chosen.

Quota Sampling

This method is popular in street surveys and opinion polls. It selects a cross-section of people based on certain factors like their age, sex and social class. Once you have determined how many people in each category you want, you keep on asking until the desired number has been achieved.

Cluster Sampling

This is when a particular group of the population is selected as the sample. This would occur, for example, if a decision was made to study the needs of children living in residential care, and a random sample of residential homes was made.

Connoisseur Sampling
This type of sampling is based on the personal recommendations of those you approach to participate in the research. Their suggestions as to whom to approach are based on their perceptions of the type of person they think you want to interview. This method is used when the task facing you is to contact difficult to reach minority groups. An example of this would be steam model railway enthusiasts, or paedophiles. This technique is used when studying networks, but raises problems of confidentiality and anonymity.

Making a Case Study
A questionnaire used initially to gather information may lead on to case studies to illustrate typical respondents. In selecting a case to study, ask the following:

● Is the case selected a typical example? Can you check this?
● Does the case demonstrate your professional competence?
● Is the case study retrospective (looking at what has already happened) or prospective (a case you will follow into the future)?
● Have you access to the records, people and facilities to complete your research?

Some non-typical cases may, nevertheless, be interesting. A *deviant case analysis* could be chosen to highlight the untypical, or a *critical incident analysis* could illustrate an unusual occurrence.

Observation and Study
Observation research can be conducted in a highly structured and systematic way, complete with observation schedules. Unstructured observation simply means keeping your eyes and ears open, and making a record of anything relevant or interesting.
    Observation is a useful tool for establishing what people actually do, as opposed to how they think they behave, or the way they describe their own behaviour. This type of research needs to

be conducted using an ethical code of conduct. It would be unacceptable, as well as illegal, to act as some kind of 'Peeping Tom', invading an individual's privacy.

The main value of observation research is to check the integrity of other data. The drawbacks are that it cannot interpret an individual's behaviour or discern his motives. The only satisfactory way to do so is an in depth interview or case study.

Interviewing

Conducting a questionnaire is like having a written conversation with someone, because it is a structured way of obtaining information.

Interviews for research purposes also need to be carefully structured, particularly when they take the form of a 'before' and 'after' survey of public perceptions, as might be carried out by the Research and Development Department of a large authority.

In a structured interview the researcher asks every person the same questions and in the same order. An unstructured interview tends to develop more flexibly, responding to the interests and preferences of the person being interviewed, and digresses to explore promising avenues of enquiry as they arise. Or you can balance the strengths and weaknesses of the two approaches.

The structured approach is likely to be appropriate when:

- the aim is to discover 'how many'
- clarity is all important
- a direct comparison has to be made between different responses
- the answers have to be converted into statistical evidence.

The unstructured interview is likely to be effective when the objective is to explore:

- a person's attitudes and beliefs
- an individual's value system
- the experience of individuals
- what influences people to reach certain conclusions.

It can take into account non-verbal communication. Interviewers – like solicitors, police and probation officers – can explore an individual's attitudes and uncover the underlying message, (ie, what they really mean, as opposed to what they are verbalising).

Here are some practical issues to consider when conducting interviews:

- *The location* needs to be accessible, comfortable and conducive to relaxed conversation with no interruptions.
- *The timing* needs to be mutually convenient and, once arranged, confirmed by the interviewer.
- *Whether the interview is recorded* needs to be clarified at the outset, as some people find the presence of a tape recorder inhibiting. The interviewer needs to be familiar with the equipment and to have checked that it works.
- *Behaving consistently* is important. It is too easy to have preferences, relating warmly to some and inhibiting others.
- *A code of practice* is useful to all participants. This should set out clearly your methodology, and cover issues such as the confidentiality of all the information obtained.
- *Quality control* can only be achieved if the information collected is consistent, accurate and reliable. There are dangers in using different interviewers to conduct the same interviews with different people. Freak results can occur if researchers are not carefully briefed to ensure they avoid leading questions, and all ask the same questions in the same way.

Meetings
Do You Really Need a Meeting?
You may be able to circumvent the need to hold a meeting by delegating work to others. Delegating authority to act can encourage initiative and avoid the need for group action.

You may consult people individually, make a series of telephone calls, or even hold a teleconference. This allows a number of people to speak to each other simultaneously without having to leave their offices. Or you could send a memorandum requesting answers to queries, use the organisation's computer system to exchange information, use e-mail, or even the Internet.

Meetings are expensive; they take people away from their workplace, incur travelling time and associated expenses. The real cost of holding a lengthy meeting which involves a large number of highly paid individuals travelling significant distances can be substantial.

Holding Meetings

If a meeting is unavoidable, make sure it has a clear purpose. It may be necessary to conduct some market research which will require the co-operation of several colleagues, and some careful planning, if you are to obtain the necessary factual evidence. Or you may need to consult a range of colleagues from different disciplines about a particular proposal, and test out its feasibility, or identify potential problem areas.

The size of the meeting should be restricted and only those who will make a valid contribution should be invited. An agenda should be prepared and circulated in advance with any supporting papers. Allocate sufficient time. Choose a venue that is accessible and convenient. Finally, consider whether or not you should chair the meeting yourself, and make arrangements for minutes to be taken.

Be very clear about what you intend the meeting to achieve. Give thought to how you intend to handle it. Make sure you have read all the relevant background papers.

Once you have welcomed everyone and made any necessary introductions, your opening statement should define the purpose of the meeting, and what outcomes you are expecting.

You need to take control at the outset, and strike a correct balance which encourages participation yet prevents anyone from dominating.

Try to stimulate discussion and involve all members. Ask general questions to encourage participation. Direct specific questions to individuals who are not contributing. Encourage everyone to share their ideas and clarify contributions by paraphrasing what has been said. Seek clarification, if misunderstandings are arising, and periodically summarise the conclusions that have been reached.

Try to avoid the following problems that can arise in meetings:

- procedural nit-picking or points of order
- confusion over what decisions have been reached
- straying from the main point
- destructive conflict as opposed to honest disagreement

- reluctance to contribute
- subversion by members who have a hidden agenda.

At the end of the meeting, remind everyone of the objectives and summarise the main conclusions that have been reached. Review the agreed action plan, making sure that individuals who are taking action forward are clear what is expected from them, and the agreed timescale. Unless the meeting is a one-off, a date for a follow-up meeting, to review progress, needs to be agreed before the participants disperse.

Following the meeting make sure the minutes record the essential facts and the main decisions reached. Circulate the minutes as soon as possible to all participants and others who did not attend the meeting but need to be kept informed. The date of the next meeting should be confirmed in the minutes and the agenda circulated later.

After the meeting pause to reflect and evaluate its effectiveness. You may wish to contact those who attended and invite them to comment.

10

SELECTING AND EVALUATING RESEARCH MATERIAL

I have chosen the contents of the Annual Policing Plan of the Hampshire Police Authority as a good example of the ground covered by this type of report. It shows the wide range of techniques involved in such a report, which has to be both comprehensive and authoritative. Here is a list of sources:

- The previous year's Policing Plan.
- The Strategic Plan for Hampshire Constabulary.
- A policy document titled 'Enforcing the Peace'.
- Her Majesty's Inspectors of Constabulary report for the previous year.
- Personnel statistics and projections.
- Demographic information.
- The most recent Census Report.
- A report titled 'A Social Mosaic of Hampshire'.
- The Home Office National Key Objectives Document.
- Crime Statistics.
- Detection figures for crimes of violence, offences against the elderly and minority groups.
- A Survey of Burglary Victims that had been commissioned.
- Crime and Incident Management Unit statistics on repeat victims.
- The results of a Harris Poll.
- Details of the Research and Development Department's surveys of public perceptions.

- Control room telephone recording system generated statistics.
- Response time statistics.
- Independent survey data carried out by the Automobile Association.
- A report titled 'The Masefield Scrutiny' which is an assessment of the administrative burden placed on the police by the Criminal Justice System.
- The Victim's Charter.
- Victim Information Point statistics.

It is an immense amount of information; all is needed to evaluate the work of the authority in a systematic and comprehensive way. The report analyses the performance achieved against both the National Key Objectives and the local Police Authority Local Objectives.

A report of this breadth and scope deploys a variety of methodologies, including sampling techniques, and must have needed many meetings.

Evaluating the Quality of Your Research

You will have to judge which combination of research techniques will make the greatest impact.

Your research will be evaluated for relevance and originality. The authority of your report will depend on the integrity of your research, which must conform to the following standards:

- It must be unbiased, objective, truthful and representative.
- The methodology must be reliable and statistically sound.
- The results must be capable of being repeated.
- The researchers must have acted responsibly, and followed a code of ethics that ensures those taking part are unharmed by the experience.

Part Four

WRITING THE REPORT

11

STRUCTURING THE REPORT

Reviewing the Terms of Reference
Your terms of reference should include:

- the subject of your report
- the scope of the study required
- a request to make recommendations, if appropriate.

Other information you should have includes:

- who requested the report, and their status/position
- who is responsible for producing the final report
- who else is involved, and their rôle
- when the finished report is needed.

Some reports are internal, and the terms of reference might read like this:

Accident/Incident 20th August (year)
Please carry out an investigation into the incident that occurred in the Press Shop when Mr J Summertime received serious injuries.

You should involve Mr N Mills, the Health and Safety Representative, in your investigation and consider whether anyone has acted negligently.

The completed report should be submitted to me not later than 31st August when it will be considered by the Board of Directors.

Other requests may be prompted, for example, by the need for information about the current level of sales. In these cases the nature of report required and the intended readers' needs are clear from the outset. Here is an example:

'Provide a report which compares the monthly sales achieved in the present financial year with the previous year's figures, for the next Planning Group Meeting.'

The terms of reference in the next example are vague rather than specific and would benefit from further clarification. The nature and scope of the enquiry required needs further definition:

'Examine the growing trend of holiday-makers to book directly with tour operators rather than use a travel agent.'

Here are terms of reference given to a Parliamentary Committee with responsibility for Human Rights:

'Examine the need for a Human Rights Bill which would incorporate the European Convention on Human Rights into British law. The following questions need to be answered:

a)   How do you ensure privacy is honoured and respected?
b)   How can freedom of expression be maintained and developed?
Report back with a series of recommendations.'

and another one:

'Examine the case for a stronger Advertising Standards Authority (ASA), with particular regard to:

a)   whether financial advertisements and marketing literature is misleading
b)   to what extent the system protects the buyer when it comes to financial advertising
c)   to assess whether the ASA has sufficient power to punish offending companies or to compensate investors and make recommendations accordingly.'

The final example concerns a Royal Commission set up by the Government to report on 'Providing for Old Age'. The commission was given explicit terms of reference:

'To examine all aspects of care for the elderly, having regard in particular to:

a)   an examination of ways to fund long-term care
b)   to consider whether the Government can provide a more generous system for the elderly than the current arrangements
c)   to examine the need for some form of compulsory insurance
d)   to evaluate the current main types of private long-term care which are financed by insurance schemes or through investment bonds

and make suitable recommendations.'

In this example the terms of reference are quite specific, and are listed in such a way that deliberately does not allow the Royal Commission discretion to deviate from them.

This precisely worded approach could prove useful in academic reports, retail employment, marketing and sales departments. Its value is that it provides for a comprehensive overview, yet breaks down the questions into easily digestible segments. This should produce a systematic analysis of all the available data and evidence, important when there is a large amount of complicated information.

Choosing a Suitable Layout

In its simplest form a report will consist of a beginning, a middle and an end. The beginning sets the scene by informing the reader what the report is all about and what it intends to achieve. The middle section is the most important part of the document where the detail of the message is delivered, and the arguments developed. A logical structure, written in clear language and organised into appropriate headings, will clarify the report's aim and ensure the reader's interest is maintained. The end must follow on naturally from the main body of the report, arrive at a conclusion, and guide the reader to a series of recommendations.

The structure will include some or all of the following:

- a Title Page
- a List of Contents
- the Terms of Reference
- an Executive Summary
- the Introduction
- the main body of the report containing the evidence you have collected
- your evaluation of the evidence and the force of your argument
- the Conclusions and Recommendations
- an Appendix
- a Bibliography
- an Index.

The size of the report will determine whether you include all these headings. However, the following basic ingredients are necessary even in a quite modest report:

- Title
- Terms of Reference
- Introduction
- Main Body of the report
- Conclusions and Recommendations.

Consider the following examples which all conform to this basic structure and layout, even though they are written for different readerships. It is important that a report keeps to a structure otherwise it will lack lucidity and forfeit reader interest.

Example 1
The report 'Privacy and Media Intrusion', which follows this structure, sets out the government's response to a consultation paper issued by the Lord Chancellor. The report analyses the contributions of interested parties and presents its conclusions in the following format:

1. Introduction
2. Regulation of the Press: Statutory or Voluntary

3.   The Criminal Law and Intrusion
4.   The Civil Law and Infringement of Privacy
5.   National Heritage Select Committee Recommendations
6.   Conclusion
      Annex A
      Annex B
      Annex C

The report commences with an introduction which gives the background to how it came to be commissioned. It develops the arguments in section 2, 'Regulation of the Press', which analyses the available evidence. It proceeds to develop the arguments and links this to an examination of the judicial system. Finally, the committee arrive at their conclusions which flow naturally and logically from the preceding sections.

Example 2
The next example concerns a report titled 'The Local Economy and Employment Plans' written by the Planning Officer for the County Council to highlight issues that need to be considered as the Authority prepares its Structure Plan and District Wide Local Plan.

This report conforms to the basic structure and layout but includes an executive summary which précises the report's findings on the opening page. Next comes the introduction, which explains the Council's legal duty to prepare a Structure Plan. It then adopts a systematic approach and examines all the pertinent factors – employment, levels of unemployment and other economic indicators – before concluding with an analysis of the problems facing the district. The report includes a comprehensive series of illustrations and tables and these are grouped together to form the Appendix.

1.   Executive Summary
2.   Introduction
3.   Employment
4.   Levels of Unemployment
5.   Other Economic Indicators
6.   Conclusion and Recommendations
7.   Appendix

Illustrations
Tables
Graphs

Example 3

A report from the voluntary organisation NACRO (National Association for the Care and Resettlement of Offenders) titled 'Women Leaving Prison' appears at first sight to be structured differently. The report is divided into chapters, rather like a book.

Closer examination reveals that the first chapter is in fact an executive summary, whilst the second chapter provides background information and is the introduction.

After analysing the problems facing women on discharge from penal establishments, the report's conclusion (which contains three explicit recommendations), is contained in Chapter 9.

Chapter 1	A Positive Strategy for Women
Chapter 2	Women in Prison
Chapter 3	Women's Prisons and Resettlement
Chapter 4	Maintaining Family Links
Chapter 5	After Prison: Support in the Community
Chapter 6	Housing
Chapter 7	Money
Chapter 8	Work, Training and Education
Chapter 9	Conclusion

Example 4

The report 'Credit Card Services' examines whether there is a monopoly in the supply of credit card services. The inquiry team considered a great deal of evidence and incorporated these contributions into a large Appendix under 24 sub-headings. Otherwise, the layout of the report is conventional except in that the authors chose to include the terms of reference, and methodology used, into the Appendix as well.

1. Summary
2. Background
3. The market for credit card services
4. Credit cards: profitability

5.   The views of third parties
6.   The views of the providers of credit card services
7.   Conclusions
      Glossary
      Appendices

Selecting the Title and Sub-title

The title page should display the title of the report, the name of the author, and the date when it was written.

Selecting a title is important. This must be clear, concise and inform the reader accurately what the report is all about. It is normal practice to include a descriptive title or sub-title, to supplement the main title.

There are pitfalls in choosing a title that is too long. Consider the example of a committee which is tasked with examining ways of improving the quality of health care provision, and developing programmes to improve primary health care:

A REPORT BY AN ENQUIRY TEAM INTO WAYS OF
DEVELOPING PROGRAMMES OF PRIMARY
CARE IN THE COMMUNITY

Whilst this is an accurate description of the committee's work it is a long-winded and ponderous title. On the other hand, the following alternatives are not only gimmicky, but misleading:

NEVER SAY DIE

LIVING FOR EVER

Although these titles attract attention, the approach is too flippant for a serious study into an important subject. It is misleading as it suggests that the author has discovered the secret of eternal life! The author settled for a title which conveyed a more balanced approach:

PROMOTING BETTER HEALTH
The Government's programme for improving Primary Health Care

The following examples are succinct titles, with supporting descriptive sub-titles.

Example 1

WORKING FOR SAFER COMMUNITIES
The Annual Policy Plan for Policing

Example 2

CARING FOR PEOPLE
Community Care in the next Decade and Beyond

Example 3

CREDIT CARD SERVICES
A report on the supply of credit card services in the UK

A report designed to influence public opinion or gain publicity for the organisation will benefit from a punchy title aimed at gaining maximum attention.

Consider the following examples:

Example 4

DENTAL DECAY
A review of Private Dental Schemes

Example 5

RACISM
A Survey of Racial Attitudes in Britain

The title page of a report has a similar objective to a book title. It is intended to catch your attention with a few well chosen words. The sub-title should encapsulate what the report is all about.

Signposting Your Intentions – the Contents Page
The purpose of the contents page is to show the reader how the report is organised, and indicate what is to come.

The contents page follows the title page. It lists the sections or chapters that lead progressively and logically to the conclusion. In this sense it signposts your intentions. A short report may not need a contents page. A long report will require both the main sections and sub-headings to be listed.

Compiling the contents page can be a useful part of the planning process. It disciplines you to identify the main sections and headings at an early stage, and organise what you intend to say into a logical sequence.

The outline structure of the report provides the basic framework for compiling a contents list. The main headings need to be turned into chapters or sections. The page numbers, which are added later, will be shown alongside.

Selecting the main headings requires care and imagination, depending on the purpose of the report. A marketing report needs eye-catching, arresting captions. A technical or investigative report needs clear descriptive phrases. The purpose is to enable readers to find their way around. Most casual readers will scan the headings to get a general idea of the subject matter. They will decide from this cursory examination how much is relevant to their needs, whether it is necessary to read the report thoroughly, and what level of concentration it will demand.

Sub-headings

One thing is certain to put the reader off quicker than anything else: pages and pages of unrelieved typescript! Plenty of headings, all included in the contents, will act as bait and encourage the reader to study the whole report. There is little point in writing first-class text if the layout is so dull that no-one can be bothered to read it. It must be inviting and engage the reader's attention.

Examples
Example 1
The following list of contents is taken from a report called 'Subsidence'. It clearly illustrates how useful a comprehensive contents section can be to the reader who wishes to examine a report systematically.

CONTENTS

A number of useful learning points can be seen in this example:

- The introduction contains the terms of reference, outlines the methodology used, explains how the study was conducted and the professional status of the enquiry team members.
- Every part of the country is approached logically and examined. Each is given an identifiable section for ease of reference and the conclusions are shared at that stage.
- The report concludes with a section outlining the lessons to be learned together with several case studies. This helps to keep the reader's interest and attention.
- The conclusion, titled '12 major recommendations', is clear and self explanatory.

Example 2

The next list of contents comes from a report published by the Office of Fair Trading called 'Buying a Used Car', which is designed as a consumer guide.

The report contains a title and sub-title but omits formal terms of reference. The introduction explains the purpose of the report, which is a guide written for people who don't know much about cars.

Although there is no executive summary in this report, the checklist at the end serves a similar purpose and succinctly repeats the main points in the guide under the following headings:

- The car's condition.
- Has it been in an accident?
- Has the car's identity been changed?
- Test drive.
- After the test drive.
- Has it been clocked?
- Is the car stolen?

The final part listed in the contents is titled 'What to do if things go wrong'. This section is equivalent to an amalgamation of the conclusion, recommendation and appendix, as it contains concluding advice and guidance, together with a series of useful contact addresses:

BUYING A USED CAR

How to get the best deal

Introduction
Contents
Before you buy
Buying privately
Buying at an auction
Problems
What to do if things go wrong
Checklist

Although considerable variations exist in the look of different reports, according to their purposes, in practice they tend to follow the same underlying format.

12

THE APPROACH:
EXECUTIVE SUMMARY
AND INTRODUCTION

Making an Executive Summary
Unless your report is very short you need to summarise the main points. The length of the summary depends on the length of the report. A short report may only need two or three paragraphs, whereas a lengthy and complex document may require several pages. The point of the executive summary is:

1. To give readers an overview of the whole report before they start to consider each section in detail.
2. To provide a résumé of the report for the reader who is too busy to read the whole report.

Writing a summary is difficult; the dilemma is deciding what to include and how much to leave out. Though it often comes near the beginning, it should only be written after you have completed the whole report. It should hightlight the main topics dealt with in the report and focus on your conclusions.

Skills Audit
Writing an executive summary demands a number of skills:

- Précis power
- Analytical ability
- Comprehension

- Evaluation
- Detachment.

The mnemonic 'PACED' is a reminder.

Précis power
This is the skill of reducing to the bare essentials the essence of the report, and the ability accurately to reflect its content, tone and emphasis.

Analytical ability
This skill enables you to get to the heart of the matter and sift out extraneous material from the essential facts, taking care over the pruning and editing of your material in order to highlight the salient issues.

Comprehension
This is the ability fully to understand a wide range of material, including statistical data and illustrations.

Evaluation
This is having the capacity to digest all this information and form correct judgments about the relative importance of different aspects.

Detachment
The ability to remain objective, and not allow personal preferences or bias to influence your analysis.

Adopting a Systematic Approach
Use this checklist:

- Carefully read through the whole report.
- Re-write any sections you consider are capable of improvement.
- Examine each section and assess its importance.
- Make a list of the key points.
- Using new language, compose the first draft of the summary.

- Check, edit and polish the draft by pruning out anything that is not essential.
- Critically examine the syntax, correcting any grammatical or punctuation mistakes.
- Review the draft summary, comparing it with the original report.
- Unless you are satisfied it is a clear and accurate summary, repeat the whole procedure.

Here are some common errors:

- *Short cuts*
  Trying to write the summary before the main report has been completed. You may think you know what you want to say, but do not start with the summary and use it as the model on which to structure the whole report.
- *Repetition*
  This happens when the writer unwittingly repeats in the summary the introduction or conclusion.
- *Verbosity*
  Brevity is the key word. Avoid being long-winded and explaining material that is contained in the main body of the report.
- *Confusion*
  Avoid confusing the reader. Summarise succinctly and logically, closely following the structure of the report.

Example 1

This executive summary is taken from a report written following an investigation into a salmonella outbreak which occurred in the North-East. A Christening party had been arranged in a public house and 130 guests had attended. In the following week 49 guests were diagnosed with salmonella enteritis food poisoning and a full-scale investigation was undertaken by Environmental Health Officers (EHOs).

The report identifies the probable cause of the outbreak: egg sandwiches. However, the quiche and pork pies were also found to be contaminated. Poor food handling practices and physical defects in the kitchen were identified as contributing factors.

The kitchen was too small to cope with the hygienic preparation of food for a party of this size. Food preparation work surfaces were badly scored by knives and other implements used to prepare food, and the joins at the edges of work surfaces were open and filled with food debris and dirt. The floor was filthy and littered with food waste, and samples were taken from several places in the kitchen for microbiological testing. These revealed the presence of salmonella at several locations in the kitchen, including the work-tops and in one of the cleaning cloths. There were no recorded temperature checks made of the refrigerator, and checks made over several days by EHOs recorded temperatures between 9°C and 15°C, compared to the legal standard of 8°C or cooler. There were nine key mistakes, any of which could have caused a food poisoning outbreak by itself. The main defects were as follows:

- cross contamination from raw food to cooked food
- poor layout and lack of space contributing to cross contamination
- catering for more customers than they could handle
- a 'cleaning' cloth which spread contamination
- insufficient refrigeration capacity
- one fridge which was not working properly
- no system in place to check the equipment was working correctly and safely
- an absence of staff training
- no proper system of cleaning routines.

The presence of all these serious faults made the likelihood of a food poisoning incident a *near certainty*.

Example 2
This example of good practice is taken from a report produced for the local planning committee about the local economy and levels of employment in the area. It manages to summarise both the theme of the paper and the main conclusions, whilst highlighting the pertinent and significant facts.

- The workforce in the area is growing in the long-term, but at a relatively slow rate.

- The number of people in employment has fallen considerably, but this cannot be explained by the rise in unemployment.
- The economic and employment base of the area is relatively small due to its isolation, and labour mobility is low.
- The small size of the local workforce means that any significant redundancies would have a proportionally larger effect on the economy.
- The area has a fairly diverse economy but this is heavily weighted towards the service sector.
- Unemployment rates are higher than national and regional levels, but are increasing at a slower rate.
- Numerous indicators show that the economy in the area lags behind other areas in the UK.

Introducing the Report
The introduction sets the scene for the reader and puts the terms of reference into context.

Some introductions may seek to explain company policy, others aim to inform and educate the reader, but all attempt to get the reader on side. They may contain a sentence which reflects the aims and values of the organisation or business, or share their Mission Statement and business philosophy.

The introduction provides an opportunity for the writer to thank all those who have contributed information, or assisted with the production of the report. Here are some ingredients found in any good introduction:

- Methodology
- Objectives
- Background Information.

The essence of this MOB approach is to answer the questions How, What and Why?

How did the report come to be written? (Methodology)
What was the purpose of writing the report? (Objectives)
Why was it necessary to research the subject matter? (Background Information)

Methodology

The methodology is a detailed description of the approach adopted. It explains how the subject will be tackled and outlines how the information will be presented. In seeking to answer the question 'How did the report come to be written?' we should examine:

- How has the report been organised?
- How has the research been carried out?

Example

This example taken from a Pre-Sentence Report written for a Magistrates Court follows a standard format and conforms to the basic MOB structure. It contains background information, sets out the objectives and purpose of the report, and outlines the methodology used in some detail.

The first part of the introduction contains relevant factual information, summarised as follows:

- An explanation of the legal status of the report.
- A statement that the material is confidential.
- The date of the court hearing.
- Personal details about the defendant.
- Details of the Probation Officer producing the report.
- A list of the offences the defendant has allegedly committed.
- Sources of information used in compiling the report.

The extract which follows outlines the methodology used.

This report is based on one office interview and a home visit to the family. During the past twelve months the defendant has been subject to a Probation Order imposed by the court on 15th May (year). In the preparation of this report I have consulted Probation records, and a Psychiatric Report prepared by the Senior Registrar of Forensic Psychiatry dated 8th January. I have also liaised with the defendant's solicitor, the Crown Prosecution Service and the District Drug and Alcohol Services.

Objectives

The objectives explain the primary reasons for writing the report. They set out the scope of the study and the intended outcomes. The objectives probably focus on the aims of the organisation or business in a given time span, and measure the performance achieved in relation to targets set.

Example

In this example, the authors ask 'What was the purpose of writing the report?' and examine:

- What are the priorities?
- What targets have been set?
- To what extent have they been achieved?

The introduction in the report 'Our Commitment to You – BBC Statement of Promises to Viewers and Listeners', reminds the reader how, during the previous year, the BBC issued a Statement of Promises which sets out 230 detailed promises to users of the television and radio services. The author reports the BBC managed fully to achieve 221 of these promises. The objectives set the previous year were concerned with programme content, editorial standards, and the consultation process with viewers and listeners.

The objectives for the current year build on this success. They concentrate on the priorities the corporation is particularly committed to achieving in the current year.

These objectives are listed under five key headings:

- to provide something for everyone
- to maintain high standards of fairness, impartiality and taste
- to provide value for money
- to improve access to our services
- to be responsive to your views.

In the current year the BBC state they are concentrating on:

- promises which tell the public of their aims as a public service broadcaster

- promises they made the previous year which were not fully achieved
- promises based on objectives the Governors have set the BBC
- issues which licence payers have raised as key concerns in their letters and telephone calls.

The Statement of Promises is encapsulated in the single sentence 'to provide something for everyone'. This effectively becomes the Mission Statement of the BBC.

Background Information
Background information may be included in the introduction to explain why the report was written. It may refer to an incident or sequence of events that caused the need for an enquiry or investigation.

In the case of an Annual Report, which is a legal requirement for a charity or company, the introduction may simply record, for example, that this is the third annual report to the shareholders. Some Annual Reports include a company profile. This contains background information about the company and its trading and business achievements to date. It may include information about the range of services provided, the product range and market share, and pertinent data about the company's assets.

Background information is often closely linked with information about the methodology used, coupled with an explanation of how the problem identified is going to be tackled.

In seeking to answer the question 'Why was it necessary to research the subject matter?' we should examine questions such as:

- Why has it been necessary to commission this report?
- Why has something gone seriously wrong in the running of the business or organisation?
- Why cannot a satisfactory explanation be provided for an incident, a change in circumstances, or the profitability of the enterprise?

Example
Consider this extract from the introduction to an investigation report concerning a serious accident that occurred at a factory.

The consequences of the accident were that serious damage was caused and production was badly disrupted, resulting in a substantial loss of revenue.

The introduction explains what happened and why the report was commissioned. It infers the possibility of sabotage or wilful damage, which has not been ruled out; hence the reference to whether a criminal offence was committed.

> This report was commissioned by the Chairman of the Board of Directors following the accident that occurred in the loading bay on Thursday 14th July, when serious damage was done to plant and machinery, disrupting production for several days. The purpose of the investigation is to establish the facts by seeking reports and explanations from those present, and from anyone who witnessed the accident. The actions of staff will be examined, and the question of whether a criminal offence was committed considered. The enquiry will review existing policy and procedures to establish whether there is a need to change working practices. The investigation will cover the circumstances that led up to the incident, the reasons the accident occurred, and subsequent actions taken to minimise the loss. The total lost production was £150,000 and damage totalled £50,000.

A More Detailed Introduction
Some introductions may include more than the bare essentials.

An examination of the Introduction to an Annual Policing Plan reveals twelve components which are listed below and identified numerically in the text. However, closer analysis reveals that these components can be re-classified under the three main headings which comprise the MOB approach (see page **127**).

Methodology

1.   Consultation with the public
2.   Consultation with groups at public meetings
3.   Inspection reports
4.   Performance review systems

Objectives

5.   The policing priorities for the year ahead are spelt out.
6.   Emphasis is placed on the authority's commitment to performance and value for money.
7.   The record of achievement is highlighted.
8.   A significant initiative is spotlighted.
9.   Progress on realising long term strategies is highlighted.
10. Target to civilianise suitable posts.

Background Information

11. Historical information and explanation is provided.
12. The legal requirement to produce an Annual Policing Plan is highlighted.

Example

INTRODUCTION
This is the third Annual Policing Plan published by the Hampshire Police Authority [11]. It is produced in partnership by the Police Authority and Hampshire Constabulary as required by the Police and Magistrates' Court Act 1994 [12]. The plan sets out the policing priorities for the year ahead [5]. It aims to inform the public about the services they can expect from their police force. It lays down guidelines within which local police commanders have produced *service plans* which set out how policing services will be delivered at the level of individual communities or groups of communities. These were produced in consultation with local Police and Community Liaison Groups [2] and with interested members of the public who have attended meetings [1]. Policing is a partnership not only with the people who are policed but with local authorities, other public services and other agencies in the criminal justice system.

The links between Hampshire Constabulary's Strategic Plan for the next 3-5 years and the Annual Policing Plan are self evident. The central purpose of the Strategic Plan remains to make the communities safer places in which to live, to work and to grow old. The force will continue to impact, through the *Enforcing the Peace* initiative, on those quality of life issues which are of most concern to the inhabitants [5].

The Authority and the Force aim to achieve the best value for money possible, whilst still maintaining a first class policing service [6]. The ways in which policing is provided and the standards by which the force delivers it are threaded through the plan.

The force was subject to a full inspection by two of Her Majesty's Inspectors of Constabulary [3], and the Police Authority is pleased to note the most encouraging report produced as a result of their visit. Their particularly complimentary comments about the *Enforcing the Peace* initiative gives the Authority and the Chief Constable the encouragement to continue a project which has the overwhelming support of the community and the police and civilian staff of the Hampshire Constabulary [8].

In support of its commitment to its employees the Police Authority regards the move to provide a more effective Performance Development and Review procedure, which will replace the current appraisal scheme, as a positive step [4].

A number of departments which provide support to the organisation as a whole have developed longer term strategies which will indicate to the front line commander and others how that particular part of the organisation intends to support them in the medium to long term, and improve the service they provide [9].

The Police Authority has continually sought to provide additional police officers at the 'front line' and is well on target to meet its own expectations of an extra 514 officers in the next three years [7].

In order that the target can be achieved at the earliest opportunity, the Police Authority supports the recent review of police posts suitable for civilianisation thereby increasing the rate at which it will move towards its target [10].

13

THE MAIN BODY
OF THE REPORT

Organising Your System

The main body of the report must confine itself to the factual evidence. Opinions, observations and speculative comments are irrelevant at this stage. Later, when drawing conclusions, deductions and balanced opinions may be in order, providing they are based on the factual evidence.

Collect together all the necessary and relevant data, using methods such as:

- conducting interviews and taking statements
- consulting experts
- examining documents, reports and other paperwork
- by visual observation of procedure and practice
- making site inspections
- carrying out surveys and questionnaires.

The report should follow a natural, logical order as it presents the evidence, the findings and the conclusions.

Presenting Your Findings

Organise the material into several chapters or sections when there is a large amount of evidence to present. Treat the subject matter in a logical way so that it divides naturally into parts.

The main section of Hampshire's Policing Plan is concerned with the Home Office and Police Authority Local Objectives and the treatment adopted is as follows:

Home Office National Key Objective 1
To maintain and if possible increase the number of detections for violent crimes.

Home Office National Key Objective 2
To increase the number of detections for burglaries of old people's homes.

Home Office National Key Objective 3
To target and prevent crimes which are a particular local problem, including drug related criminality, in partnership with the public and local agencies.

Home Office National Key Objective 4
To provide high visibility policing so as to re-assure the public.

Home Office National Key Objective 5
To respond promptly to emergency calls from the public.

Police Authority Local Objective 1
To improve the quality of life of residents by tackling threatening, intimidating and anti-social behaviour through the Enforcing the Peace Initiative.

Police Authority Local Objective 2
To reduce road collisions, particularly those which are serious and fatal.

Police Authority Local Objective 3
To ensure that those members of the public who wish to be advised of the initial outcome of their call to the police are promptly informed of the result.

Police Authority Local Objective 4
To improve the service provided to victims of, and witnesses to, crimes by:
- keeping them informed of the progress of cases throughout the criminal justice process, from arrest to final disposal

- encouraging the prompt submission and better quality of files submitted to the Crown Prosecution Service.

This framework is helpful to the reader as it presents the information logically and without ambiguity. In this report the significance of the information and the trends are explained, with statistics and facts being illustrated with graphs and other pictorial techniques.

Analysing the information takes place once it has all been collated. Often the analysis is interwoven with the facts, and interpretation is provided as the argument develops.

Each section of the report is tackled using an identical framework. This makes it consistent and user-friendly. As an example, let us look at 'Home Office National Key Objective 1'. This section begins by setting out three key factors:

- *The National Key Objective*
  To maintain and if possible increase the number of detections for violent crimes.
- *The Performance Indicator*
  The number of violent crimes detected per one hundred officers.
- *The Target for the Current Year*
  To maintain the number of detections of violent crimes at 180 for every 100 officers in the Constabulary.

This gives the section focus and the report takes shape naturally with the findings grouped under logical headings. This links with the overall objectives, and enables the report to flow smoothly.

These three key factors are next dealt with under the following headings:

- The Performance Indicator in perspective
- The current position
- How this objective will be achieved
- Alcohol and violence
- Domestic violence
- Young people and violence
- Racial abuse and violence
- Violence against children

- Rape and sexual assault
- Violence against old people
- Abuse and violence against gay and lesbian people
- Violence in context.

Now we take as a detailed example the section of the main report headed 'Alcohol and Violence'. The writer identified a need for three sources of information (referred to by number in square brackets in the extract):

1. Statistics on the total volume of crime in the County for the last year.
2. A breakdown of the crime figures showing where alcohol was a factor.
3. Policy documents which set out the Constabulary's approach to 'alcohol related violence'.

ALCOHOL AND VIOLENCE

Alcohol is known to be a major factor in offences involving violence against the person [1]. Figures for last year indicate that either the offender, the aggrieved or both had been drinking at the time of, or immediately prior to an assault in 41.6% of reported cases [2].

The Constabulary will adopt a three pronged approach to reduce the level of alcohol related violence [3]:

- *education*
  by working with schools to educate children and young persons regarding the effects and potential dangers of alcohol abuse and how to adopt strategies to avoid being assaulted.
- *enforcement*
  by targeting licensed premises where breaches of the licensing laws regarding supply and consumption of alcohol are known or suspected to be taking place, and by high profile policing in areas where those under the influence of alcohol are likely to congregate.
- *multi-agency co-operation*
  by working with local authorities, licensing justices

and the licensed trade to reduce the opportunity for alcohol related violence to occur. By pursuing 'Enforcing the Peace' initiatives help to provide long term alternatives to alcohol consumption and misuse.

Evaluating the Evidence

For this you need good organisation and effective time management. Do not become bogged down with piles of paperwork, some of which may be peripheral or irrelevant. I hope you will not discover important research has been omitted and insufficient time remains to rectify the shortfall!

Anticipate objections to the arguments being advanced, and be prepared to meet them head on. Tackle issues systematically so that reader interest is maintained. The argument will flow if proof can be provided at appropriate points. Skilled use of data can be persuasive in winning over the reader to your point of view. Develop your arguments carefully and move steadily towards your conclusion.

The Office of Fair Trading report 'Buying a Used Car?' shows how this can be done. It splits the main body of the report into two.

The first half concentrates on the three main ways a vehicle can be purchased second-hand:

- buying from a dealer
- buying privately
- buying at an auction.

The second part of the report is headed 'Problems'. The main difficulties that can arise are researched and grouped into:

- Mechanical condition and safety.
- Stolen cars.
- Does the car belong to a credit company?
- Clocking.

We will consider the section on 'Stolen Cars'. The information sources are highlighted by the bracketed numbers in the extract as follows:

1. Crime statistics published by the Home Office.
2. A practical guide to the law affecting motorists.
3. Vehicle Registration Document V5.
4. Information obtained from the Driver and Vehicle Licensing Agency (DVLC).
5. Interview with representative from a police force.
6. Interview with representative from an insurance company.

STOLEN CARS

Half a million cars were *stolen* last year. Over a third were *not recovered* [1].

If you buy a stolen car, the police can take it from you to return to the original owner, or the insurance company if a claim has been paid. You will not get any compensation even though you bought the car in good faith.

You can sue the seller for your losses but this might be difficult if you bought privately and the seller has disappeared. If you bought the car on credit you may still have to pay off the loan. It depends on the type of agreement you have [2].

It can be hard to tell whether a car is stolen. Its identity may have been changed. For example, the identity number and number plate of a legitimate car may have been transferred to a stolen one. Vehicle registration documents can be forged or obtained by fraud. But there are tell-tale signs to look out for. Ask to see the vehicle registration document (V5) [3]. If the seller can't produce this document, be suspicious. A common excuse is that it has been sent to the DVLA (Driver and Vehicle Licensing Agency) for updating. This may be true, for example, the seller may have changed address recently. But be wary. It means you cannot check the car's ownership and identity details.

The seller should have a green slip if the car was bought very recently and the V5 is with the DVLA for the change of ownership to be recorded. This only applies to cars that have been issued with new V5s, introduced in March 1997 [4].

Are there any spelling mistakes or alterations to the V5? If so, it may be a forgery. All legitimate V5s have watermarks.

Ask for proof of identity and address such as a driving licence, passport, recent gas or electricity bill. Check that the same name and address is given on the V5.

All cars have three main identifying features [5]:

- the vehicle registration mark (the number plate);
- the vehicle identification number (VIN) – this can be found on a metal VIN plate, usually in the engine compartment, and stamped into the bodywork under the bonnet and the driver's seat. As a security measure some cars have the VIN etched on their windows or lamps;
- the engine number.

These are shown on the V5. The numbers on the car should be the same as those on the V5.

Have the identification numbers been tampered with? The engine and VIN numbers may have been interfered with. Areas of glass may have been scratched off the windows, or stickers may cover up etching which has been altered.

Another clue is whether the seller can show you the insurance policy for the car. If it is stolen, probably not [6].

Use the checklist to help you spot the signs of a stolen car.

The extract introduced the statistical evidence about the scale of the problem, followed by advice on how to check the ownership of a vehicle. The argument advanced in this section is be suspicious and wary, otherwise you may have cause to regret it. Use the three point check list before parting with your hard earned money!

Deciding on Your Priorities

Information has to be prioritised, highlighting the main matters, and relegating insignificant details to their proper place, which may mean leaving them out altogether! You may need to commission illustrations to add emphasis and clarity.

Review the material and check the following:

- Has it been organised systematically and clearly?
- Does the sequence of events emerge coherently?

- Do any of the facts contradict each other?
- Have any irrelevancies crept into the report which need eliminating?
- Is there information missing that should be included?
- Is there a need to conduct any further research?

In a Pre-Sentence Report written for the Magistrates' Court, information collected by the Probation Officer has to be reviewed and prioritised. The material is obtained by interview, examining case records, and from contacting other agencies with knowledge of the individual and their family.

The middle section is structured around:

- The Offences
- The Risk to the Public of Reoffending
- Personal Circumstances of the Offender
- Response to Previous Supervision.

Each of these sections is broken down into further sub-headings:

- *The Offences*
  a) Examines the defendant's recollection of the alleged offences and the circumstances.
  b) Describes in detail the defendant's involvement in the offence that has led to this court appearance.
  c) Explores his reaction to the offence, including his attitude and whether he feels any remorse.
  d) Sets out his overall view of the offence and his perception of how the Court are likely to view his behaviour.
  e) Offers a professional perspective of the situation in relation to the offences and the effect on the victim.

- *Risk to the Public of Reoffending*
  a) Describes his previous record of offending.
  b) Outlines the seriousness of his criminal record and offers some explanation for his behaviour.
  c) Gives an account of previous efforts made to combat his offending behaviour.
  d) Explains what problems he has faced and whether he has been able to overcome them.

e)   Describes any mitigating circumstances.

- *Relevant Information about the Offender*
  a)   This covers his marital status, domestic circumstances and accommodation arrangements.
  b)   employment status and financial circumstances
  c)   childhood experiences and early conflict with the Law
  d)   physical condition
  e)   personality factors and an assessment of his mental health.

- *Response to Past Supervision in the Community*
  a)   Advises about any previous statutory supervision.
  b)   Recalls any non-compliance with the terms of supervision.
  c)   Gives information about any custodial history.
  d)   Describes his attitude to supervision and supervisors.
  e)   Assesses the likelihood of future co-operation if a further community based sentence is made.

Once satisfied all the information is accurate, review whether the correct emphasis and interpretation has been given. Tailor the language appropriately to the intended readership. When writing an important document like a court report, or a report for an industrial tribunal, the tone used in the report needs to be kept formal and respectful. Confirm the impression that you are a professional person, with knowledge, integrity and judgment!

The example which follows, although fictitious, is based on the *Relevant Information about the Offender* section of a report actually presented in court.

The defendant is a single man who lives in local authority accommodation which consists of a one bedroom flat. He states that he has recently become reconciled with his girl-friend, but the success of this depends on his remaining clear of drugs. Mr 'T' has been unemployed for the past two years. He is dependent on long term sickness benefits of £55 per week, but is waiting for disability payments to be reintroduced which will increase his income. The rent for his accommodation is paid for by Housing Benefit. Other outgoings include HP payments of £10-50 per week for domestic items.

Mr 'T' appears to have had a normal childhood until the age of fourteen when he learnt that Mr 'T' senior was not his father. This appears to have had a devastating effect on him. A deterioration in his behaviour occurred which resulted in him being placed in a residential school for children with behavioural problems. Shortly afterwards he first came into conflict with the law and progressively developed a pattern of persistent offending. The defendant has abused drugs and alcohol for many years which has increased his propensity to aggression.

Five years ago the defendant was involved in a fight and received a blow to his head which rendered him unconscious for ten days. Medical reports indicate that the defendant suffered residual effects of visual disturbance, dizzy spells, irritability, loss of temper and mood swings. He also experienced some physical impairment to his right arm and leg. Mr 'T' continues to experience some problems relating to that injury and recently was treated by his General Practitioner for depression. Currently he is prescribed benzodiazepams to assist him in sleeping.

Earlier this year the defendant appeared before the Court and a medical report was compiled by Dr 'F', Consultant Forensic Psychiatrist. He expressed an opinion that Mr 'T' was not at the time suffering any mental illness but had a life long personality disorder characterised by antisocial behaviour and episodes of impulsive behaviour, instability in relationships and a relative lack of remorse. His personality disorder had been further compounded by the illicit use of drugs. It was also indicated there seemed little evidence of any motivation to change. He was subsequently sentenced to three months in custody and was released on the 17th May (year).

14

TECHNICAL MATTERS
AND DATA

Technical Matters

Technical matters require special treatment for a non-technical
readership. Otherwise the report will not be understood, like this
one:

This new portable desktop computer is being marketed with
the following technical specifications in a magazine which
has a wide general readership.
- 150MHz up to 166 MHz.
- Large 12.1" screen.
- 16MB of RAM upgradeable to 80MB.
- 1.08GB up to 5.1GB hard drive.
- Integrated diskette, hard drive and CD-ROM drives.
- 4Mbps infrared communications.

This information is incomprehensible to a non-technical reader.
None of the features is explained in terms of the value of the
product to the entrepreneur, businessman, homeuser or student,
who are the intended buyers. As a marketing document it fails to
promote the product effectively.

The basic structure of a technical report is similar to any other.
The skill lies in presenting technical issues, such as, for example,
specification details, essential mathematical data, symbols and
working models. All these have to be explained clearly. Tables

and statistics may go in appendices at the end.

The following extract from a scientific report expresses mathematical and temperature data, yet clearly demonstrates how to set out

- percentages
- temperature fractions
- dates
- weights.

CARBON EMISSIONS

By the year 2012 world emissions of carbon dioxide are set to rise by 30 per cent. The result would be annual worldwide emissions of 8200 million tonnes of carbon, an annual increase of 1700 tonnes in 15 years.

Average global temperatures have risen 0.6°C since the Industrial Revolution and could be set to rise a further 0.6° unless calls to curb emissions are heeded.

Selecting a Suitable Style

Do not slip into jargon, or make phoney use of language which sounds academic. Avoid errors like the following:

A new product line is experimentally developed using a range of techniques, selecting a variety of variables and assumptions before arriving at a satisfactory outcome.

All this actually says is 'a new product is developed'.

Technical or unfamiliar terms should be explained clearly. Here is a good example of a report that contains scientific material but caters for a non-technical readership. In this extract about deuterium gas, mathematical percentages are expressed in a user-friendly way and unfamiliar technical terms are carefully explained.

An international team of astronomers observing the absorption spectrum of a quasar through the Hubble Space Telescope, found the fingerprint of deuterium. The gas cloud contained approximately 2 deuterium atoms for every

10,000 hydrogen atoms, which is a density ten times higher than observed elsewhere.

This indicates that the total mass tied up in baryons, which is the ordinary matter which forms stars and planets, is between 1 to 2 per cent of the 'critical mass' needed to stop the Universe expanding.

The next example is an extract from a report on measuring atoms which is a complex subject and of limited interest to the general reader. The author tackles the subject in a way that is readable and clear. It is stripped of all technical jargon and is an excellent example of technical report writing.

ATOMS

Atoms will flip between energy states if they are hit with radiation at the resonant frequency.

In caesium, the nucleus and outermost electron spin rapidly generating minuscule magnetic fields. The spin of the electron and nucleus can be in parallel in which case the fields repel each other. If they are anti-parallel they attract. The jump between these two spin states is called a hyperfine transition and is how we define a 'second'.

A second has a resonant frequency of 9 192 631 770 oscillations of this radiation.

Incorporating Mathematical Data
There are no hard and fast rules about whether to use numbers or words, but clarity and visual appeal are the main considerations.

- Avoid commencing a sentence with numbers.
- Use words when estimating a number or series of numbers.
- Use numbers for addresses, dates, diagrams, figures and page numbers.
- Avoid using two numbers in succession if possible. It is better to describe an engine which 'has four cylinders producing 60 hp'.

Mathematical calculations pose special problems and need to be displayed on a separate line for reasons of clarity. Normal typesetting can be used for a simple algebraic formula as follows:

$$\frac{(a + b) - c}{5}$$

More complicated algebraic expressions may need to be written out separately and later incorporated into the report, unless special typesetting facilities are available on your word processor or computer.

The mathematical formula shown in figure 1 relates the length of a pendulum (g) to the time it takes (T) to swing from one end of its arc to the other end and back. The row of dots at the end denotes that there are an infinite number of other terms in an ascending order of even powers to the value of sin $\frac{1}{2} \propto$.

$$T = \pi^{1} \sqrt{\frac{1}{g}} \left\{ 1 + (\tfrac{1}{2})^{2} \sin^{2} \tfrac{1}{2}\alpha + \left(\frac{1.3}{2.4}\right)^{2} \sin^{4} \tfrac{1}{2}\alpha \ldots \right\}$$

Fig. 1

Do not write out complicated formulae by hand unless the report is to have only a very limited circulation. Use commercially available lettering guides, stencils or transfers which look more professional.

Tables
Use a table to present statistical information or complex technical details. Whether it is tables of financial data on interest rates, stock market movements, population statistics, or data showing the maximum loading a component can handle, the information must be capable of being readily absorbed.

Headings should be unambiguous and laid out across the page. This makes it easier for the eye to follow. Columns of numbers are easier to assimilate than trying to absorb figures which run horizontally across several columns.

A timetable for a Ferry Service demonstrates this point quite clearly. This information is readily absorbed:

Weekdays	Weekends
0045	0050
0330	0700
0600	0830
0740	1000
0830	1115
0910	1230
1050	1400
1215	1530
1355	1700
1500	1850
1615	2030
1730	2150
1830	2300
1940	
2050	
2200	
2300	

Now look at this one:

Weekdays

0045			0330		
0600	0740	0830	0910	1050	
1215	1355		1500	1615	1730
1830	1940	2050		2200	2300

Weekends

0050					
	0700	0830		1000	1115
1230		1400	1530		1700
1850		2030	2150		2300

Exactly the same information is shown in horizontal form. It is logically coherent, but less easy to follow. Avoid this type of muddled layout.

Most businesses lay great emphasis on forecasting cash flow and profit & loss. They need an accurate picture of how the business is progressing. This data forms the basis on which finance is negotiated and is an integral part of the business plan.

The next example shows how to set out a simplified profit and loss forecast for the quarterly period 1 January to 31 March.

	JAN	FEB	MAR
SALES	850	850	700
less Direct Costs			
Raw materials	165	165	125
Labour	180	175	110
Total Direct Costs	345	340	235
GROSS PROFIT	505	510	465
less Overheads			
Rent and rates	100	100	100
Heat and lighting	25	25	25
Telephone	120	110	85
Stationery	40	40	30
Administrative staff	100	100	80
Depreciation	65	65	65
Other	75	55	55
TOTAL OVERHEADS	525	495	440
NET PROFIT	-20	15	25

Quantitative Data

Data can be classified as either quantitative or qualitative.

Quantitative data can include material such as:

- demographic information
- financial information
- results of questionnaires or surveys
- statistics.

Statistics and numerical data can be persuasive if presented carefully. Most people have a healthy respect for such information as it is perceived as authoritative.

Care should be taken over the presentation of statistical data.

All numbers should be checked for accuracy by two different people, and the layout carefully aligned so that nothing can be misinterpreted.

Do not be tempted to massage the figures if your research throws up an unexpected result. Never rely solely on one set of figures or a single reading. Double-check all your statistical evidence by taking several readings and cross-checking the results critically.

Quantitative data can be more effectively presented using bar charts, pie charts, histograms, pictograms or graphs. These are eye-catching and fun to look at and the information they contain is more easily absorbed by the reader. See Chapter 16, page **158**.

Qualitative Data
Qualitative data is material such as:

- transcripts of answers given in open interviews
- notes of observations you have made
- photographic evidence or pictures
- related documents which may be included in the appendix
- detailed descriptions of scientific experiments.

Enhance the presentation of qualitative data with techniques like spidergrams, flowcharts and pyramid diagrams. (These are explained on pages **165** and **169**.)

Use your qualitative data to identify your key findings, then marshal your evidence and make your point with conviction.

Subject to privacy considerations, it is legitimate to use direct quotations from tape-recorded interviews, provided the exact words are used and the speaker is acknowledged. It is good to use specific and relevant quotations to support a key point you are making. This has more impact than a litany of general observations.

15

CONCLUSIONS AND RECOMMENDATIONS

You are about to finalise the main findings section of the report. Before considering what conclusions to draw, check again the quality of your data.

This should be done systematically:

1. Compare and cross-check the information you have gathered with material from other sources to avoid ambiguity and contradictions. Constantly ask yourself, 'How reliable is this information?'
2. Re-examine the terms of reference and check that each point has been fully addressed.
3. Compare your findings with those from previous studies to guard against inconsistency.
4. Test out your findings with some of the people interviewed and gauge their reactions. Usually the participants are willing to give you the benefit of their experience. Honest feedback is invaluable.
5. Check carefully that the findings logically point to the conclusion you are going to draw. Consider whether any alternative rational explanations fit the facts. It may be that more than one solution is viable. Now is the time to discover and evaluate alternative answers, not when you have put the finishing touches to the final report.
6. Consider whether you may have influenced the conclusions yourself by using biased methodology. Examine all the

assumptions you have made. Do not let personal values and beliefs colour your judgment.

Arriving at Conclusions

The conclusion is where the writer provides a précis of the findings of the report.

The final arguments are drawn together and each possible solution is considered on its merits. It is here you weigh up the strengths and weaknesses of the alternatives and evaluate the potential of each.

The purpose of the conclusion is to sum up succinctly the sense of the main body of the report, and, if appropriate, formulate recommendations. These should flow naturally from the conclusion. They should come as no surprise to the reader if you have written your report with care, as he will already have been led to anticipate them. Certain types of report may not require recommendations. For progress reports, or most other routine reports, recommendations would be superfluous.

Every writer should aim to end the report on a positive and up-beat note. An investigation should conclude with a suggestion about how the problem can be resolved. A proposal should finish with a series of recommendations which inspire confidence.

Avoid false endings, unnecessary repetition or long-windedness. Be crisp. The conclusion is your golden opportunity to influence the reader decisively.

In this example the Licensing Panel of a local authority has received an application for a Dangerous Wild Animal Licence in order to run an ostrich farm. The committee have asked their official to prepare an assessment of the merits of the application for the next meeting.

The official considers two letters of objection, inspects the site accompanied by the Council's Veterinary Inspector and then has discussions with the applicants.

In his report the official evaluates the merits of the application before reaching his conclusions. He is not expected to make any formal recommendations. That is seen as the prerogative of the Licensing Panel, but he uses the Conclusion section to indicate clearly how best to deal with the application.

The application for the granting of a Dangerous Wild Animal licence has merit providing the legitimate concerns of the objectors and the Council's Veterinary Inspector are given due weight.

Subject to the following conditions being imposed it would be reasonable to grant a Dangerous Wild Animal licence:

a) a solid barrier be erected alongside the boundary with Station Road;

b) the inner fence be raised to a height of 2 metres;

c) that adequate warning notices be erected;

d) proper fire fighting equipment be placed on site;

e) arrangements be made for 24 hour on site supervision;

f) that a mains water supply be provided;

g) that an escape gap be incorporated under internal fences;

h) that applicants, and relief staff, attend relevant courses and seminars;

i) the maximum number of animals be restricted to 6 adults, 40-60 chicks up to 6 months, and 20 chicks up to 1 month.

A reasonable time scale to comply with these conditions would be within the next three months, should the Panel consider them to be appropriate.

Making Recommendations

The recommendations should be specific and clearly identify how a particular problem or situation can be resolved.

Before starting, check once again the original terms of reference which constitute your instructions. Make sure that all angles have been fully explored.

Just as the main body of the report should develop in a logical way and lead into the conclusion, so, too, the recommendations should emerge naturally from the conclusions. Again, there should be no surprises in store for the reader. So reconsider your recommendations in the light of the following:

● Have they emerged logically from the conclusions?

● Are they consistent with the terms of reference?

● Do they link naturally with the main part of the report?

- Can you justify the recommendations you are making?
- Have you listed each recommendation separately and numbered them clearly?

The next example is taken from a report titled 'Shrinkage and Wastage'. The report was commissioned by a retail chain who asked a firm of management consultants to research to what extent the fall in profits was attributable to "shrinkage" and "wastage". The focus of their study centred on damage to stock caused by customers, the level of shoplifting, and employee theft. The conclusions and recommendations are reproduced below.

CONCLUSION

Shrinkage is well above the national average. It is costing our retail chain nearly 2½% of turnover, which is £2 million per annum.

This study is able to identify clearly the main ways that shrinkage and wastage are occurring.

- *Theft by employees*
  Employee theft is on the increase and accounts for 60% of the losses and includes the following abuses:
  a) discount selling to customers who are friends
  b) fraudulent refunds to non-existent customers
  c) key copying, this allows after hours theft to take place
  d) over enthusiastic staff who arrive early and leave late
  e) abuse of the staff discount system
  f) stock losses from the warehouses.

- *Shoplifting by customers*
  Shoplifting is a significant problem and the abuses we detected as most prevalent are:
  a) smuggling goods out of stores using 'Fagin's pockets' and 'poachers' pockets'
  b) theft using the 'booster box' technique
  c) switching labels and prices on goods

d)   exchanging old goods for new in the fitting rooms
e)   slipping goods into carrier bags bearing the company logo, in the store
f)   creating a distraction at the checkout enabling goods to be slipped into the customer's shopping bag.

- *Damage to goods on display*
Accidental breakages by customers are currently paid for by the company. The cost of this practice, coupled with the high level of shop soiled goods which are caused by customers carelessly handling delicate items, amounts to almost £200k per annum of lost revenue.

- *Human errors, staff carelessness and lax management*
This covers a range of problems which includes the following:
a)   complicated shop layouts with display areas which are difficult to supervise
b)   stores with multiple entrances and exits making surveillance difficult
c)   staff carelessness results in damage to stock and till errors
d)   management crime, includes managers falsifying the accounts, the fraudulent setting up of credit accounts, and corrupt practices in collusion with some suppliers.

RECOMMENDATIONS

We recommend a number of measures are taken immediately to combat this serious situation. If our recommendations are accepted and implemented, they would reduce losses to under £1million per annum. Although the initial cost would be £800k, the running costs in subsequent years would fall to £350k per annum, which constitutes excellent value for money.

1. Install Electronic Point of Sale (EPOS) systems in all stores linked by computer to the warehouses/store rooms to monitor all stock movements.
2. Use hidden video cameras and closed-circuit television to monitor store rooms and warehouses 24 hours per day.
3. Hire uniformed security staff to detect shoplifters and deter dishonest staff.
4. Employ 'honesty shoppers' to look out for signs of leakage in stores.
5. Increase audit checks in all stores.
6. Instruct supervisors to carry out more frequent checks, including random stock checks.
7. Standardise store layouts.
8. Introduce a policy that all damage and breakages attributable to customers are paid for by them.
9. Adopt a policy of prosecuting all shoplifters.

Including Appendices
The appendices are a reference section for the report, providing further information. They can include detailed statistical data, graphs, tables and working mathematical examples together with source documents or relevant correspondence. They amplify the text and provide additional analytical data for the serious reader.

To include detailed statistical material in the main body of the report is distracting. It interrupts the smooth flow of the developing argument. Highly technical data and long detailed material should always go in the appendices.

Attention should be drawn to the appendices at the appropriate point in the text. This can be done with footnotes or reference numbers.

Anything included in the appendices (or elsewhere in the report) which refers to another writer's work, should be acknowledged and credit given, irrespective of whether or not the author's work has been published.

Any reference to a published work should include the following biographical details:

• author's surname and initials
• the title of the work, book or article

- name of publisher
- the date of publication, which edition and the page numbers.

If the report is to be widely published, then permission for the use of copyright needs to be sought, and may have to be paid for.

16

HOW TO ILLUSTRATE
YOUR REPORT

Illustrating your report adds impact; a picture is worth a thousand words. A report uses words to get its message across. However, diagrams, bar charts, graphs and drawings can increase the visual appeal and clarify the meaning. Illustrations can do more than replace the need for lengthy and tedious explanations. They can enable complex information to be conveyed accurately and vividly.

The following questions should be addressed:

● What information should be presented visually?
● Will an illustration prevent confusion and help the reader to understand the point you are trying to make?
● Is the diagram relevant?
● Which is the best approach to use to present the information?

The most common formats used for presenting information in diagrammatic form are:

● tables
● bar charts
● pie charts
● graphs.

You need to understand the relative strengths of these different formats so as to decide how information is best presented.

Police Strength

TABLE 1

Rank	Number of Officers in post ten years ago		Number of Officers in post currently		Estimated Number of Officers in post next year	
	F	M	F	M	F	M
Chief Constable		1		1		1
Assistant Chief Constable		4		3		3
Superintendent		41		39		36
Chief Inspector		56	1	46	2	45
Inspector	3	129	7	150	7	149
Sergeant	12	426	29	449	45	466
Constable	239	2188	448	2174	501	2223
Sub-total Female/Male	254	2845	485	2862	555	2923
Total	3099		3347		3478	

Civilian Strength
Full Time Equivalent

TABLE 2

Number of Civilian Staff in post ten years ago		Number of Civilian Staff in post currently		Estimated Number of Civilian Staff in post next year	
Female	Male	Female	Male	Female	Male
Not available	Not available	869	533	897	558
Total full time equivalent 1072		Total full time equivalent 1402 (inc 239 part time)		Total full time equivalent 1455 (inc 259 part time)	

Fig. 2 Tables showing police strength:
   Table 1 Officers
   Table 2 Civilians

Computer programs are available on many office systems to help draw them up.

Tables

The simple use of tabular format was discussed on page 147. Rather more elaborate tables convey a great deal of information precisely but they need to be carefully interpreted.

The tables in figure 2 (page 159) are taken from the "Annual Policing Plan for Hampshire" and show the actual numbers of people who were in post, or expected to be in post on these dates. These figures vary depending on the number of people who retire or leave at particular times. They represent the actual strength of the Force, not the approved establishment.

Bar Charts

Facts and figures can be presented in a more eye-catching form by using a bar chart. For example, the Government publishes

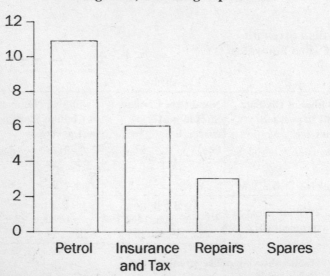

Fig. 3 A basic bar chart.

up-to-date statistics on an enormous range of topics, which can be consulted and the data used to construct your own graphs or bar charts.

A bar chart has several advantages over a table:

- it is more striking
- it highlights the comparatives more clearly
- it saves time, as the information is easily understood and digested.

Keep it simple, or these advantages are lost.

The bar chart in figure 3 shows the average weekly amount motorists spend on running costs (excluding depreciation). It is easy to see that the largest item is fuel, almost as much as the rest put together!

Figure 4 shows at a glance by looking at the heights of the

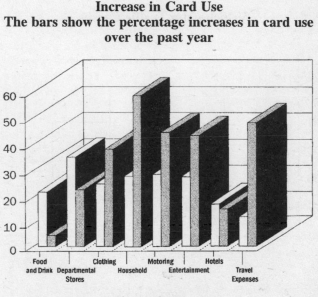

Increase in Card Use
The bars show the percentage increases in card use over the past year

Credit cards   Debit cards

Fig. 3 A bar chart comparing Credit and Debit Card usage.

bars, that debit card use is growing faster than credit cards for household items and travel expenses. For food and drink it is the other way round.

A histogram is a type of bar chart which illustrates frequency of distribution.

Figure 5 displays the ages of the drivers of vehicles at a traffic census. The smallest number of drivers were found to be in the '17-20' age range. The second smallest number were in the 'over 60' age range.

This example has a further feature which is useful. It uses the width of the bar to reflect the size of the range. Thus the standard age range, which covers a ten year period, is represented by standard width blocks (20-30, 30-40, 50-60), whilst the narrowest age range (17-20) and widest age range (over 60) require blocks of a different width.

Vehicles at a Traffic Census

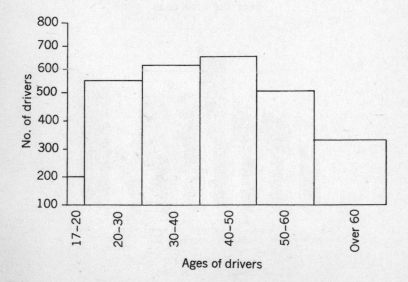

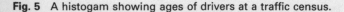

Fig. 5   A histogam showing ages of drivers at a traffic census.

Pie Charts

A pie chart looks like a circle divided into a number of slices. It shows the size of each slice as a proportion of the whole. Pie charts are most effective when the number of slices used does not exceed six. You calculate the size of the slice by reference to the size of the angle subtended at the centre of the slice. The total circle is 360°, so a 10% share would be 36°, a 25% (one quarter) share 90°, a one third share 120°, etc.

Figure 6 illustrates the percentage of households who have the use of vehicles (many cars are owned by companies but kept and

Percentage of Households with Vehicles

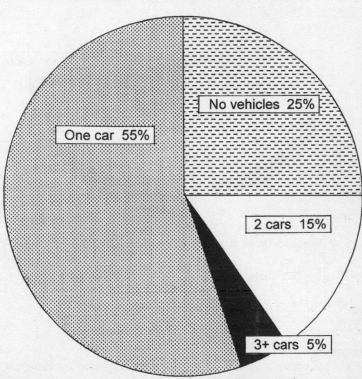

Fig. 3 Pie chart showing vehicle availability by household.

used by employees). The pie chart shows that 75% of all households have at least one vehicle, and 25% of households are dependent on public transport.

The pie chart in figure 7 outlines the Council's anticipated income in the coming year. It reveals the largest contribution, 41.5% of the total, comes from Government grants.

Where the Money Comes From

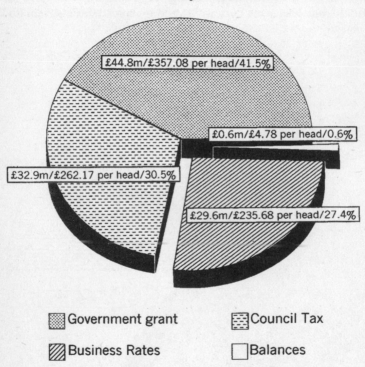

£44.8m/£357.08 per head/41.5%

£0.6m/£4.78 per head/0.6%

£32.9m/£262.17 per head/30.5%

£29.6m/£235.68 per head/27.4%

Government grant Council Tax

Business Rates Balances

Fig. 7 A pie chart showing sources of Local Authority finance.

Graphs

While bar charts are ideal for displaying things that are different, a line graph is better for showing a measurement of something that continues, enabling the reader to focus on the overall trend rather than the specific data. It can have two or more lines (better not to have too many) enabling the reader to compare different sets of data in the same graph. Different lines should be in different styles, e.g. dotted lines, dashes, solid lines etc., or different colours can be used.

Figure 8 compares the record of housebuilding starts by housing associations, private builders and local authorities over half a century. The graph clearly shows a dramatic fall in local authority building compared with the private sector, which has fluctuated considerably. On the other hand, housing association provision, whilst steady, is relatively insignificant.

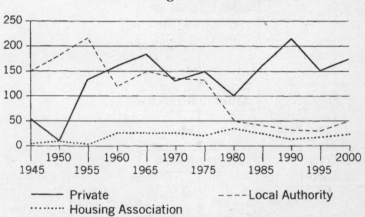

Housebuilding Starts 1945-2000

Fig. 8   A multiple line graph showing a comparison of private, local authority and housing association housebuilding starts over half a century.

Flowchart
A flowchart expresses a complex scenario of possible events and options in a coherent way.

Figure 9 describes the steps involved in seeking employment.

Applying for a job

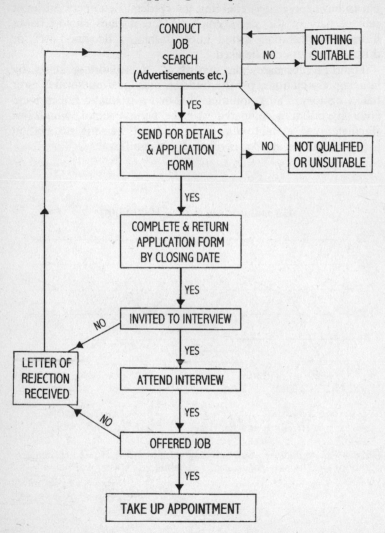

Fig. 9   A flowchart.

Organisational Charts

These are frequently used to describe the structure of a hierarchy, clarify the lines of authority, and describe the professional relationships between different staff within a department, both vertically and horizontally.

These family trees show the formal channels of communication and the status of different employees. What they cannot show is the *informal* structure. This is the power and influence that individuals wield due to force of personality, networking skills and specialist knowledge.

Figure 10 shows the top management in a manufacturing company. It shows the areas of responsibility of the five senior managers who comprise the management team and are accountable to the Chief Executive.

The Hierarchical Structure

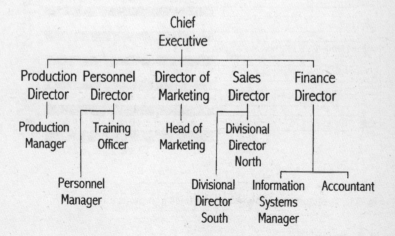

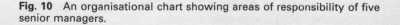

Fig. 10 An organisational chart showing areas of responsibility of five senior managers.

Pictograms

Pictograms (pictorial diagrams) are the oldest form of communication and go back thousands of years to the time when people painted symbols on the walls of their caves.

Examples today include some road signs, symbols of men and women used outside public toilets and labels on clothing giving washing instructions.

Where the Money Goes

SERVICE	GROSS EXPENDITURE £000's	LESS INCOME £000's	NET EXPENDITURE £000's	
EDUCATION	52,330	7,673	44,657	
SOCIAL SERVICES	17,719	6,104	11,615	
HIGHWAYS	5,443	276	5,167	
POLICE	10,309	5,184	5,125	
FIRE	4,027	32	3,995	
PLANNING & ECONOMIC DEVELOPMENT	549	0	549	
RECREATION & TOURISM	969	216	753	
REFUSE DISPOSAL	1,940	407	1,533	
OTHER SERVICES	8,850	4,014	4,836	
TOTAL	102,136	23,906	78,230	

Fig. 11   A pictogram showing the Council's expenditure

Figure 11 shows how the Council plans to spend its budget on the various services it provides. It uses pictograms to represent the various services, for greater impact.

Cartograms

A cartogram is a map which provides comparative information about different areas by superimposed figures, symbols or shading.

It can be effective and economical, and can combine well with charts and pictograms.

Figure 12, "Weather Forecast", uses cloud symbols obscuring the sun to show it will be cloudy yet bright. Arrows indicate the direction of the wind, and temperature figures symbolise predicted temperatures. Rainy clouds are used to inform readers that the expected weather in the West of Scotland will be cool, wet and windy.

Spidergrams

A spidergram is where you start with a central theme and radiate ideas from it, so that the finished diagram resembles a spider's web.

Its main value is to help the reader to visualise graphically how qualitative data is organised.

The process starts by identifying the main theme which you draw in the centre of the page. Next you add lines which radiate outwards from the centre, each one leading to a different idea, or highlighting the relationship with the central theme, as shown in the example overleaf.

In figure 13 the Community and Social Services Directorate have taken on additional responsibilities for the Housing Service and propose to set up a "Specialist Services and Professional Audit Unit". This pivotal role is highlighted more effectively in this example than by a more conventional organisation chart.

A Pyramid Diagram

A pyramid diagram is another technique which can be used to identify certain types of pattern in your data. Figure 14 shows one which exemplifies a view of the structure of a business.

Weather Forecast

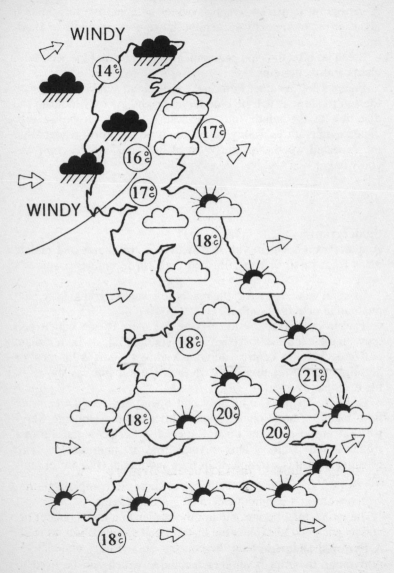

Fig. 12 A cartogram.

Proposed Specialist Services and Professional Audit

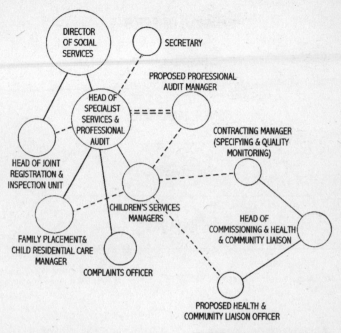

SOURCE: 'NEW HORIZONS' REPORT

Fig. 13 A spidergram.

Providing Technical Illustrations and Artwork

The purpose of illustrating technical writing is to complement the written word and communicate a technical message.

The writer may be introducing the reader to a new concept or product and need to explain the features and specification, as well as convey the ideas behind the concept, in a readily understood form.

Illustrations and drawings can be presented in a number of ways:

Company Structure

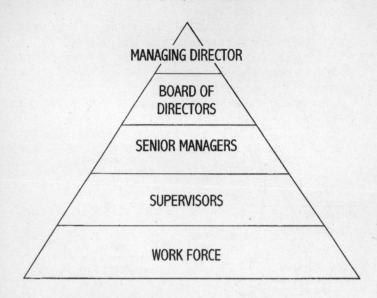

Fig. 14 A pyramid diagram.

- *Orthographic drawings* are a true plan and elevation of an object which is drawn to the correct scale and are used for design or manufacturing purposes.
- *Isometric drawings* are used by technical authors and engineering draughtsmen for illustrative purposes. They show in a single diagram the length, breadth and thickness of an object. This avoids using the traditional plan, front and side elevations approach which necessitates three separate drawings.
- *Perspective drawings* give an impression of an object, but they lack the realism and geometrical accuracy of an isometric drawing. They are often produced by draughtsmen with limited artistic skills.
- *Line drawings* are the most common form of technical illustration and are used when the demand is for a sketch of a piece of equipment under development. Shading can be

applied to improve the appearance or to emphasise a particular feature of the product.

- *Half-tone drawings* or natural photographs can lack technical detail but be more realistic than line drawings.
- *Colour* can be employed to good effect if used sparingly.
  Colour printing is more expensive but the use of separate
  colours, on a graph for example, can make it easier to
  understand the relationship between different sets of inter-
  secting curves and values.

Tinted paper can be an effective way to highlight pages of
technical drawing. It is also less costly than colour printing.

Part Five

A FINAL EXAMPLE

17

AN INVESTIGATION IS CONDUCTED

An investigation is undertaken when a serious incident or accident occurs and it is important to establish exactly what happened.

The repercussions from an incident may include handling potentially damaging publicity that can affect the reputation and profitability of the business. It may also lead to a claim for compensation and damages where serious injuries or death have occurred. Issues of culpability need to be examined and the possibility of criminal negligence explored.

Statutory agencies and public bodies which are directly accountable to the public are well aware of the political implications.

Companies, businesses and financial institutions who provide goods and services can be in an invidious position if they do not comply with relevant legislation like the Food Safety Act or the Sale of Goods Act. Selling a product that is faulty and causes harm to a customer can lead to prosecution and result in a claim for compensation. Those providing services must not contravene the Trades Description Act or Consumer Protection Act.

If an accident occurs in the workplace there is usually an investigation to establish whether the employer has failed in his duty under the Health and Safety at Work Act 1974 to ensure, as far as is reasonably practicable, the health, safety and welfare at work of their employees.

The employer's duty of care includes ensuring the following:

- safe arrangements and working methods
- safe work premises
- providing suitable materials and equipment
- appropriate training and supervision of staff
- competent staff.

Initially, when an accident occurs at work the relevant supervisor will complete an Accident Report. This should give an account of the incident, outline the circumstances and the nature of the injury sustained. An independent report from a doctor is necessary.

As soon as possible, an investigation into the circumstances surrounding the accident should take place.

A Case Study

An accident occurs in a hotel kitchen and results in a catering assistant sustaining serious injuries to his hand which he placed inside a food mixer. The injuries require 18 stitches, and he is admitted to hospital for three days.

Following the accident the victim's solicitor writes to the employer, claiming negligence and failure in their duty of care to the employee. The basis of his claim is that his client was using a food-mixing machine which was unguarded. The solicitor requests an opportunity to inspect the machine and take photographs, which is granted, as he intends to pursue a claim for compensation.

The accident investigator starts by identifying a need for the following information:

- A medical report which describes the injuries and details of the treatment, including hospitalisation.
- A copy of the employee's training record containing details of all formal training he has been given, including safety instructions he has received on the food mixer.
- Statements from anyone who witnessed the accident.
- Evidence about whether the machine was used without a guard.
- Information concerning whether the machine is in good working order and regularly maintained.

- The full service history of the food mixer, including checking out if there have been any problems previously.
- An assessment about whether the accident was avoidable, and if so, who should be held responsible.

The investigating officer is given reports prepared by the doctor, the Catering Supervisor and other staff on duty at the time. The statements made by the catering staff reveal no-one witnessed the accident. A copy of the Employee Training Record is made available and the service record of the food mixer reveals it was recently serviced and pronounced in excellent working order. All the staff who provide statements are interviewed and he draws a plan of the hotel kitchen (figure 15) to clarify what happened, where, when, and how.

After conducting his investigation and sifting the evidence the investigating officer decides to rely on the following evidence:

- statement from the doctor
- statement from the Catering Supervisor
- copy of the Employee Training Record.

The hotel management arrange for a doctor to examine the injuries and his report falls into three distinct sections:

- how the accident happened
- the injuries sustained
- the treatment and recovery process.

STATEMENT FROM DOCTOR

The patient sustained an injury to his right wrist whilst working in the hotel kitchen. He informed me that he placed his hand inside the mixing machine whilst trying to retrieve a block of butter that he had dropped into the machine. He stated he knew about the dangers he was exposing himself to, and was responsible for the injuries he had sustained.

The extent of his injuries were extensive lacerations to the web between his thumb and index finger, with the injury extending into the muscles of his thenar eminence.

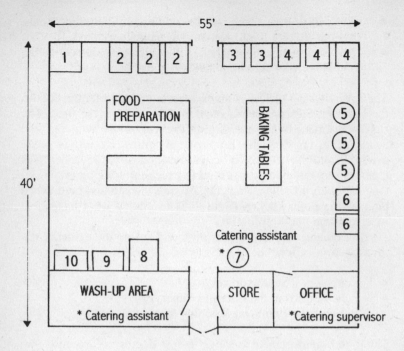

Fig. 15   Scale plan of hotel kitchen.

Key: 1   Blast chiller

2   Lainok multi-purpose ovens

3   Brat pans

4   Deep fryers

5   Boiling pans

6   Steamers

7   Food mixer (Industrial Wondermix)

8   Grill pan

9   Cookery range

10   Vectair oven

First aid was given on the spot and a compression bandage applied, then he was taken to the local Casualty Department for treatment. That evening he underwent surgery under general anaesthetic to repair the damage to his hand. Fortunately it was found that he had sustained no permanent damage to major nerves or blood vessels in the hand. He was discharged from hospital on the 29th June and considered fit to return to work on the 16th July.

The Catering Supervisor provides a statement which comments on three aspects of the accident:

* factual information about the mixing machine
* details of the employee's training record
* an account of the action taken following the accident.

STATEMENT FROM THE CATERING SUPERVISOR

The mixing machine is an Industrial Wondermix model which does not have a guard over the bowl.

This caterer has not received training in how to operate this machine correctly. He should not have attempted to operate or use the machine without supervision. His training record clearly shows which items of equipment he has been trained to operate. Once he has been fully trained to use a particular piece of equipment he signs the training record, and is permitted to operate the equipment without supervision.

The accident had already occurred before I arrived on the scene. I applied first aid to the victim using a compression bandage, until he could be taken to hospital for treatment.

The Catering Supervisor also provides a copy of the employee's training record which lists the items of catering equipment he has received training to operate without supervision. This list does not include the Industrial Wondermix however. His training record includes the following signed statement which is explained to each employee before they sign the form.

EMPLOYEE TRAINING RECORD

The correct operation of the machines listed overleaf has been fully explained to me and I understand:

1. I must not operate a machine which has a guard provided, without that guard being in position.
2. Before cleaning or adjusting any electrically operated machine it must be isolated from the electricity supply, by either removing the plug from the mains or switching the machine off at the main switch.
3. Protective equipment must be worn at all times, including safety boots.
4. I must not clean or operate any machine until I have been instructed how to operate and maintain it correctly.

Signature
Full Name
Date

The Accident Report

The investigating officer receives clear terms of reference. These require him to investigate the incident formally and write a report within 14 days. The company are anxious to establish the facts and seek advice from their insurance company's solicitors about whether compensation could be an issue.

The investigating officer establishes a systematic approach to conducting the investigation. The methodology he adopts, which I have called the 'SPIDER' approach, is designed to answer the questions, What, How and Why.

- *What* was the sequence of events and what are the facts?
- *How* did the incident or accident occur?
- *Why* did it happen and could it have been prevented?

The Spider Approach

- *S*ite Inspection – Carry out a site inspection and make a record of anything that has been removed from the scene of the incident.

- *P*hotographic Evidence – Obtain photographic evidence, if possible, of the accident scene including any suspected faulty equipment.
- *I*nterviewing Witnesses – Obtain written statements and interview all witnesses, clarifying any discrepancies in their statements.
- *D*rawing a plan – Draw a scale plan of the area showing clearly the position of all the witnesses.
- *E*vidence gathering – Obtain corroboration of witness statements. This can be from other witnesses (although be wary of collusion), or from independent sources. Obtain an independent Medical Report or an Engineer's Report, the Employee Training Record, a Health and Safety Risk Assessment, an Environmental Health Officer's Report and the Service Record relating to the equipment.
- *R*eview the data – This is where the evidence is collated, prioritised and evaluated, prior to drawing conclusions and forming a judgment about culpability.

A detailed and factual draft report is prepared which ensures the data is accurate and seeks corroboration of witness statements wherever possible.

After checking the draft for accuracy the final report is prepared. The tone should reflect the fact that it will be sent to the company's solicitors, who need an objective Accident Report if legal proceedings are instituted by the victim.

THE INDUSTRIAL WONDERMIX ACCIDENT

The Terms of Reference
To investigate how an employee received injuries from a food mixer whilst working in the hotel kitchen.

Introduction
On the 26th June (year) an accident occurred in the hotel kitchen when a catering assistant received serious injuries to his hand when he placed his hand inside an Industrial Wondermix food mixer. Statements were received from other staff working in the kitchen at the time, together with a report from the Catering Supervisor and a doctor. All

witnesses were interviewed, a copy of the employee training record was obtained and the service record of the Industrial Wondermix inspected.

Executive Summary
The accident was a consequence of the Catering Assistant placing his hand in a food mixer to retrieve some butter he had accidentally dropped into the machine. He was not trained to use the machine and should have sought assistance from his supervisor. The employee acted recklessly and is entirely responsible for the regrettable accident that occurred.

The Findings
The injured Catering Assistant joined the company three weeks prior to the accident on the 1st June, and had undertaken washing up duties in the kitchen.

The sequence of events was as follows: the employee was carrying out his normal washing up duties when he was asked to move some boxes of butter to the kitchen stores. As he was passing the food mixer he stopped to rest the box on the side of the mixer which was in use and unattended. He accidentally dropped one of the packets in the mixer and, anxious not to ruin the food that was being mixed, put his hand in quickly and tried to retrieve the butter whilst the machine was still running. Unfortunately his wrist snagged on the side of the bowl and his hand was crushed as the mixing paddle was turning.

His injuries were fairly serious and are detailed in the Medical Report included in the Appendices. He suffered extensive lacerations to the web between his thumb and index finger. Doctors inserted 18 stitches into his hand and he was admitted to hospital as an in-patient until the 29th June. Fortunately he made a full recovery and suffered no permanent damage, returning to work on the 16th July.

For the purpose of this enquiry I have checked the service record on the food mixer, and contacted the service engineer who states the food mixer whilst old is in excellent order. He suggests that when the time to replace it arrives the company obtain a model with a built in guard.

Conclusions
This accident was regrettable but could have been avoided if our employee had exercised more care and taken basic precautions to safeguard his own health and safety.

The Catering Assistant should not have been in the vicinity of the Industrial Wondermix food mixer as he has not been trained to operate it. Due to an unfortunate set of circumstances a packet of butter he was carrying slipped from his control into the food mixer which was left momentarily unattended.

This mixer does not have a guard over the mixing bowl. Whilst this is not to imply the machine is unsafe, it does indicate the need for vigilance and training before working in the vicinity of this piece of equipment.

The only member of staff on duty who had received First Aid training was the Catering Supervisor. He acted promptly, correctly administering First Aid, then taking the casualty to hospital for treatment in his own car.

Recommendations
1. The Industrial Wondermix is replaced with a food mixer with a guard over the bowl once replacement is necessary.
2. The Catering Assistant receives full pay for the period he was unable to work due to this accident.
3. The Catering Supervisor is commended for his prompt action in administering First Aid.
4. All catering staff to receive First Aid training.
5. Liability for this accident should not be admitted on the grounds that everything reasonably practicable under the Health and Safety at Work Act 1974 was done.

18

THE FINAL PRESENTATION

Presentation

Clearly you cannot send a report off as a collection of loose papers hoping someone will arrange them into a semblance of order. The pages must be attached together in the correct sequence. Options are:

- A simple report of a couple of pages may only need a staple or two to hold it together.
- A longer report could be placed into individual transparent covers and placed in a ring binder with the title printed on the cover.
- A more permanent way is to bind the report using a plastic or wire ring binder and place it in a transparent plastic cover so the title can be seen clearly. This is the best if a lot of copies are needed.

If the report is lengthy and complex you may need an index. This is compiled by selecting the key words and references in each section, and arranging them in alphabetical order with the relevant page number alongside.

Numbering the pages is important, in case a page becomes detached. Start at number one for the first page, and carry on sequentially.

For numbering the sections and paragraphs, use a decimal point type of system. Divide the report up into its principal sections. Let us suppose, for example, that there are four. These principal sections would be numbered 1. to 4. Then consider the paragraphs or sub-sections within each principal section. Suppose there are two in the first section, nine in the second section, three in the third section and four in the last. Then the numbering scheme would be:

1.1 1.2
2.1 2.2 2.3 2.4 2.5 2.6 2.7 2.8 2.9
3.1 3.2 3.3
4.1 4.2 4.3 4.4

Circulation of the Report

Send a brief covering letter or memorandum out with the report reminding the reader why it was written. In the case of a consultation document, invite a response in the form of comments by the required date. Or you may need to stress the need for action by a certain date and perhaps include an action plan. This can draw colleagues' attention to their obligations in a helpful way.

When sending a report by post consider in what state it is likely to arrive. A heavy document in a flimsy envelope invites trouble. Ensure the postage applied is correct for the weight. If time is of the essence, consider using First Class Post, special delivery, or even a courier.

INDEX

RIGHT WAY
PUBLISHING POLICY

HOW WE SELECT TITLES

RIGHT WAY consider carefully every deserving manuscript. Where an author is an authority on his subject but an inexperienced writer, we provide first-class editorial help. The standards we set make sure that every **RIGHT WAY** book is practical, easy to understand, concise, informative and delightful to read. Our specialist artists are skilled at creating simple illustrations which augment the text wherever necessary.

CONSISTENT QUALITY

At every reprint our books are updated where appropriate, giving our authors the opportunity to include new information.

FAST DELIVERY

We sell **RIGHT WAY** books to the best bookshops throughout the world. It may be that your bookseller has run out of stock of a particular title. If so, he can order more from us at any-time – we have a fine reputation for ''same day'' despatch, and we supply any order, however small (even a single copy), to any bookseller who has an account with us. We prefer you to buy from your bookseller, as this reminds him of the strong underlying public demand for **RIGHT WAY** books. Readers who live in remote places, or who are house-bound, or whose local bookseller is uncooperative, can order direct from us by post.

FREE

If you would like an up-to-date list of all **RIGHT WAY** titles currently available, please send a stamped self-addressed envelope to ELLIOT RIGHT WAY BOOKS, BRIGHTON RD.,
LOWER KINGSWOOD, TADWORTH, SURREY, KT20 6TD, U.K. or visit our web site at www.right-way.co.uk